Cherished

365
DEVOTIONS THAT CELEBRATE GOD'S LOVE FOR YOU

Kim Crabill

BroadStreet
PUBLISHING

BroadStreet Publishing Group, LLC
Racine, Wisconsin, USA
BroadStreetPublishing.com

Cherished: 365 DEVOTIONS THAT CELEBRATE GOD'S LOVE FOR YOU

Stock or custom editions of BroadStreet Publishing titles may be purchased in bulk for educational, business, ministry, fundraising, or sales promotional use. For information, please e-mail info@broadstreetpublishing.com.

Cover design by Chris Garborg at garborgdesign.com.
Interior design and typesetting by Katherine Lloyd at theDESKonline.com.

Printed in China

17 18 19 20 21 5 4 3 2 1

Brenda, my most Cherished-
when I saw the name on this
book I knew it was the one
I wanted for you. Theres NO way
in the world I can express all
that you mean to me. we have
been through so much together &

For all those who need a daily reminder
of what my grandfather told me:
"As much as I love you, there's One who
loves you so much more, and He is
with you wherever you go."

you have always been there for me.
I can't imagine my life without
you in it. we may desagree
but the love never changes. You
are the strong & steadfast sister
God knew I needed & I am so
thankful for. My prayer for you
is that God will continue to bless
& keep you in His loving arms & protection
for many years to come.

Happy 80th Birthday To
a very remarkable Lady.

My Love to you dear
Sister always.
Charlotte

Introduction

The best part of my day is in the early morning when it's just God and me, talking and listening to each other. And often, the next best part of my day (apart from enjoying my husband and sons) is when I get to share with another woman (or two … or two hundred) about what I discovered from God that morning.

That love of connecting with like-hearted women led to these devotionals. Many of them started out as simple e-mails I would shoot out each morning to a few friends. The few multiplied, and now I hope we can multiply the connections even further with this bound compilation.

I want these daily readings to help you take your eyes off the day's demands for a few minutes and focus on the God who loves you more than you can imagine. I want them to open your eyes to how active and personal God is in your life. And I want them to show you the joy of recognizing and responding to daily opportunities to encourage others as God grants you the courage.

You will find an action prompt at the end of each devotional, but most of the time I do not suggest what to write. In another place (a diary, notebook, or electronic file) you may want to journal a prayer of response, an idea you want to pursue further, or the name of a friend you want to call. There's no limit to what you and God might come up with!

Blessings,
Kim Crabill

Calm Inside and Out

I keep my eyes always on the LORD.
With him at my right hand, I will not be shaken.
—PSALM 16:8

Are you anticipating the new year with excitement? Calm? Worry? Dread?

As I ponder this question, I'm reminded of a particular baseball game. My youngest son, Austin, was five or six and playing first base when the opposing team's batter hit a pop-up. The ball looked as if it was going to the moon before beginning its descent. With two outs, Austin needed to make the catch to secure the win and the championship. He stood calmly, glove poised, and *made the catch!*

After the game, I applauded him for his cool confidence in a difficult situation. "Wow, Austin," I began, "what a great job you did! I would have been scared, but you were so calm out there." Looking up at me, his eyes revealed the struggle he had overcome. "I may have been calm on the outside, Mommy, but I was shaking on the inside!"

Does life sometimes make you shake on the inside? Just as Austin kept his eyes on that fly ball, you can face the new year with determination by keeping your eyes on God's great promises and unchanging love.

Sharp Words

The word of God is alive and powerful.
It is sharper than the sharpest two-edged sword, cutting
between soul and spirit, between joint and marrow.
It exposes our innermost thoughts and desires.

—HEBREWS 4:12 NLT

Have you ever wondered why people act as outrageously as they do? One reason is the absence of God's Word in their lives.

The Bible is not a dead old book. It is active! When we read it and do what it says, God's Word transforms us from the inside out. It tempers us, calms us, and aligns our will to God's. It introduces us to Jesus Christ who saves us from our selves and transforms us into the people God created us to be. So when we see people behaving in a way that shocks and offends us, let's pray someone will lead them to the Word. Because if not for the Word, then we might be acting the same way.

If you haven't already done so, find a Bible, an app, or a written plan that allows you to read through God's Word this coming year.

The Perfect Plan

For we are God's handiwork,
created in Christ Jesus, to do good works,
which God prepared in advance for us to do.

—EPHESIANS 2:10

My foundation was shattered at age four as I was snatched from the only home I had ever known. I wasn't who I thought I was. I wasn't where I thought I belonged. I began to lose myself in a tumult of unanswered questions. Looking back, I realize the moment you lose who you are, you start to become the person everyone else perceives you should be. The moment you lose what you thought you were supposed to do you begin to do what everyone else expects that you should do.

No one told me, "God has a plan for your life," or, "God knows you through and through and thinks you're a masterpiece." But praise God, in His perfect timing I learned the truth of both of those powerful statements. And there I found the "me" I had lost.

Are you hyperfocused on becoming who others expect you to be? Have you lost your sense of purpose because you've let others load their purposes on you? It's never too late to find yourself again. Begin each day by asking God, "What is your plan for me today?" In that plan, you will find the woman God created you to be.

More Ahead

"For my thoughts are not your thoughts, neither are
your ways my ways. … As the heavens are higher than
the earth, so are my ways higher than your ways and my
thoughts than your thoughts."

—ISAIAH 55:8–9

God has gone to great lengths to make Himself known
to us. His creation speaks to us about who He is. (For
starters, He has a sense of humor: consider the platypus.) His
Son lived among us on this earth to show us what God is
like. Prophets and preachers and former fishermen wrote the
words that God's Spirit gave them, and those words—the Bible—speak in great detail to God's nature and purposes.

And yet, we have barely scratched the surface. Every new
day holds the possibility of a new insight into our heavenly
Father. This is the delightful tension we live with as God's
children: that He reveals Himself to us, and yet He is too big
and mysterious and awesome for us to ever fully grasp.

*Today, thank God for something you've already discovered
about Him. And thank Him, too, that there's still much to
learn.*

January 5
Making Preparations

"Speak, LORD, for your servant is listening."
—1 SAMUEL 3:9

If spending time with the Lord daily is a new practice for you, these ideas may help.

Prepare your schedule. Commit to a quiet period each day to read and reflect. It can be five minutes or fifty minutes. You need to *schedule* this time because you will never "find" the time.

Prepare your space. Commit to a specific space—anywhere quiet and private. Keep your Bible, a pen, and a personal journal (if you use one) in that space.

Prepare your curiosity. Asking questions can help you personalize the Scriptures and learn more deeply. What does this passage say? What issues does this passage address? What does this passage teach me about God? What does this passage teach me about me? What does God want me to learn, change, or do because of the truth in this passage?

Prepare your will. Commit to do whatever you sense God is asking you to do.

Prepare your heart. Some people read a favorite psalm, some pray, some may read a devotional. Listening to a praise song or hymn can also help you move into a worshipful mode.

How do you quiet your racing mind for Bible study? How do you stick with it even when it seems as if God is silent?

By Name

"He calls his own sheep by name."

—JOHN 10:3

What is your mailman's name? What's the name of the young man who delivered your firewood? What is the name of the saleswoman who helped you find that elusive birthday gift for your teenage son?

There's something very personal and powerful in hearing someone call you by your name. *Jesus* calls you by name. The moment you met Him, He wrote your name in His book of life. And He thinks of you every moment in a deeply personal way, by name.

We are never more like Jesus than when we are valuing people as highly as He does. Today surprise some folks by using their name. Notice how they respond. What does it do to their countenance? Something miraculous happens when we notice people the way Jesus does.

Dear Lord, you are my Shepherd and I am your sheep. Thank you for calling me my name. When I stray, you gently nudge me back onto the right path. Teach me to follow you and walk in your ways, today and always.

Messes Welcome

"I have loved you with an everlasting love;
I have drawn you with unfailing kindness."
—JEREMIAH 31:3

After days of cleaning and yard work, Lee and I finally had everything perfect for his parents' visit. I told our toddler, Trey, to sit tight, then ran upstairs to touch up my makeup before they arrived. A few minutes later, I heard unfamiliar sounds. *Swoosh. Thud. Swoosh. Thud.* What in the world? Rounding the corner, I looked down to see the biggest smile ever on Trey's little face.

He showed me his surprise. "Look, Mommy. I brought you a flower!" Trey had tried to pick a day lily. Instead, I guess because it had been newly watered, the entire plant popped right out. A lot of things could have gone through my mind, but my thoughts were overwhelmed by sweet eyes, a loving heart, and a grand gesture meant to make his mommy smile.

Dear friend, consider my heart toward my toddler, then imagine the heart of God as He looks upon you today. He could never be disappointed as you strive to please Him. He looks way beyond the works of your hands to the love in your heart. With that great truth in mind, you can move into your day with the confidence of a dearly loved child.

Blurred Vision

Be not conformed to the pattern of this world,
but be transformed by the renewing of your mind.

—ROMANS 12:2

Have you ever been plagued with blurry vision? Usually the condition passes quickly, but if it persists, you can get confused about where you are, what time of day it is, and more.

Our spiritual vision can get blurry too at times. I've noticed several common indicators of a blurred spiritual vision: We try to do everything because we can no longer discern what God wants us to do. We rationalize iffy behavior. Areas that once seemed black and white to us now seem gray and "not so bad." We procrastinate because we've said yes to so much that we don't know where to begin. We look for truth in the wrong places: TV, horoscopes, self-help books, popular opinion.

Thanks be to God, we don't have to stay in that condition. We simply need to shift focus to our Father as He is revealed in our Bibles. One of the roles of Scripture is the "renewing of your mind" (Romans 12:2), which is another way of saying it clears up our blurry vision and puts our focus where it needs to be.

Where is your focus today? What are some practical ways you can allow the Holy Spirit to renew your mind, instead of being "conformed to the pattern of this world"?

Sing Along

He put a new song in my mouth.

—PSALM 40:3

f your life were a song today, what would it be titled? "Rainy Days and Mondays"? "I'll Do It My Way"? Or perhaps "I Wanna Talk about Me"?

It's easy to sing a song someone else has written. But did you know God has given you your own song? That song is the praise that arises in you when you think about what He has done in your life. What is your heart singing today? How has God been good to you? What painful places has He healed? How has He rescued you? What has He changed about you for the better?

Whatever song you sang in the past, God has given you a new song for today. Sing it!

Journal about a spiritual song or hymn that affected your approach to the day. Then write a few verses unto the Lord, using Psalm 40:3 as a model: "You put a new song in my mouth, a hymn of praise to you, our God. Many will see and fear you, Lord, and put their trust in you."

Young on the Inside

Praise the Lord … who satisfies your desires with good
things so that your youth is renewed like the eagle's.

—PSALM 103:1, 5

A woman had a near-death experience. On the gurney, going into surgery, she asked, "God, is my time up?" And He said, "No, you have another forty-three years, two months, and eight days to live."

Once this woman recovered from surgery, she figured she might as well look her best for this long life still ahead of her. So she had liposuction, a tummy tuck, a facelift, and a few other procedures. She looked amazing! Upon leaving the hospital, she was crossing the street when a bus came from out of nowhere, and the next thing she knew she was at the Pearly Gates. Hands on hips, she said to God, "You told me I had forty-three years, two months, and eight days left to live. Why did You let that bus hit me?"

And God said, "Well, honestly, I didn't recognize you."

I can't resist a joke! But it's no joke that we often focus so much time, expense, and energy on rejuvenating our outsides that we forget to rejuvenate the inside too.

What can you do today to rejuvenate your heart and soul?

Listen to Yourself

The tongue has the power of life and death.
—PROVERBS 18:21

We know how crucial it is for us to use our words carefully in our dealings with others. We know the potential for good and for harm our words possess. But when is the last time you really paid attention to the words you speak to and about *yourself*?

Our self-talk also holds the power of life and death. A conversation full of words of regret or blame or shame can be death to your spirit. In contrast, words that give courage, that dwell on how you're learning and growing, that are grounded by confidence in God's sufficiency—those words give life.

Many of us are stuck in the rut of automatically talking negatively to ourselves. But we can train our brains to avoid the old, negative messages we've been listening to and choose instead a new, positive message. That's how God made our brains to work.

For one day, write down what you find yourself saying to yourself. Did you rehash a past experience that you wish you had handled differently? Maybe you recalled words from a parent or a teacher, words that may have been intended to be helpful, but you didn't take them that way. Or maybe your inner conversation was full of doubts that you could handle a looming challenge. Start retraining your brain by writing down one life-giving message to tell yourself this day.

What to Pray for Yourself

We continually ask God to fill you with the
knowledge of his will through all the wisdom
and understanding that the Spirit gives.

—COLOSSIANS 1:9

I've heard it said that prayer is not what we do to change God's mind; rather, it's what we do to align ourselves with His mind. In his letter to the Colossian believers, the apostle Paul packs some powerful prayers into just a few verses. He gives us a pattern for how to pray for our believing friends *and for ourselves.*

In Colossians 1:9–12, we learn to pray that

- God will help us know what to do and be.
- God will give wisdom and understanding from His Spirit.
- God will help us live to please Him.
- God will make our lives fruitful.
- God will give us more knowledge of Him.
- God will give us strength, endurance, and patience.
- God will give us a spirit of joyful thanksgiving.

The focus of these prayer requests is on God's purposes, not our own. I'm convinced we have not even begun to experience what is possible when we pray this way.

Do you ever wonder if there's something more to pray for yourself beyond "Help me not to snap at my husband today"? Write out a few prayers using Colossian 1:9 as a model.

Why Am I Here?

Each of you should use whatever gift you
have received to serve others, as faithful stewards
of God's grace in its various forms.

—1 PETER 4:10

Not long ago, I had a CT scan. When I got to the hospital, I was *not* doing my happy dance. I was sitting there thinking, *Really, why am I doing this? I'm healthy. I have a thousand other things I want to do today.*

Finally, I regrouped mentally and asked, "OK, God, am I here for a reason? Am I supposed to learn something from someone? Am I supposed to give something out to someone else? You have my attention. I'm focusing less on me now and more on you. I want to hear you."

Across the room sat a lady looking terribly tense. So I asked her, "Are you OK?" And the tears came. "They think I have pancreatic cancer," she said.

I put my hand on hers and said, "I don't know what's going on with your diagnosis, but I know this: I can pray for you. Would you like to pray?" We had the most special moment together. Afterwards I told God, "You are so good, even in the moments when I am too into myself and my schedule. Thank you for showing me how to serve those around me today."

*God has entrusted each of us with a way of touching lives.
What encouragement needs to come out of your mouth today?*

Within Reach

> Now what I am commanding you today is not too
> difficult for you or beyond your reach. It is not up in
> heaven, so that you have to ask, "Who will ascend into
> heaven to get it and proclaim it to us so we may obey?"
> Nor is it beyond the sea, so that you have to ask,
> "Who will cross the sea to get it and proclaim it to us
> so we may obey it?" No, the word is very near you;
> it is in your mouth and in your heart so you may obey it.
>
> —DEUTERONOMY 30:11–14

For the longest time, I would awaken each morning to near panic, certain I was going to miss God or not find His plan that day. If you have ever had a similar spiritual panic attack, then Deuteronomy 30:11–14 may help you as it has helped me.

You see, God did not come to conceal but rather to reveal His plan to us. We don't have to worry that we will miss Him. God promises all of us today that He will put within us what we are to do. That's God's part, and all that's left for us to do is to find the courage to obey.

Lord, reveal your plan for me today, and grant me the courage to walk it out.

It's in the Bag

"Then you will know the truth,
and the truth will set you free."
—JOHN 8:32

We all carry around brown paper bags filled with our hurts and tragedies and disappointments and addictions. Sometimes we try to pretty up our bags with our busy little lives, our happy little smiles, and our peppy little personalities. But no matter what we do, we know we're carrying around a bag full of burdens. I know this is true because I carried around a bag like this for more than twenty-five years.

These bags and their contents eat away at us no matter how cleverly we try to deny their existence. They nibble at our confidence. They gobble up our peace. And that leads us to the big question: *What's in your bag that's eating away at you?*

Now, I can guess what your first response to that question would be. "I'm fine. I'm fine. Nothing is eating at me!" But unless we address that question, we are stuck. We will miss the miracle of God turning those brown-bag burdens into blessings.

Take a moment to ask, What's in my "brown paper bag"?
Then allow God to speak truth into your hurts, tragedies,
disappointments, and addictions.

Running Ragged

"I have come that they may have life,
and have it to the full."

—JOHN 10:10

My mom's final words to me were, "Don't live like I'm dying." She had completely lost herself in always trying to please everyone else, to take care of everyone else. She never really took the time to sit and ask, *What is my life about? What is my God-given purpose and passion?*

When we don't know who we are, we try to become everything that everyone else expects us to be. When we don't know what God's calling is on our life, we find ourselves doing whatever everyone else thinks we should be doing. And we run ourselves ragged—all in the hope that people will believe we are "fine, just fine."

Either response robs us of our true selves and keeps us from the abundant life that God has for us.

What passion have you neglected because it didn't match what you think others expect from you? Ask God to give you the courage and opportunity to take a step toward that passion today.

Not Your Job

When I am weak, then I am strong.

—2 CORINTHIANS 12:10

I have a whimsical towel hanging in my kitchen that reads, "It's exhausting being this perfect!" While intended to be lighthearted, that quip accurately describes the heaviness I felt from years of living behind a wardrobe of masks so no one would know how far short of perfection I was.

The apostle Paul wrote, "But he said to me, 'My grace is sufficient for you, for my power is made perfect in weakness.' Therefore I will boast all the more gladly about my weaknesses, so that Christ's power may rest on me. That is why, for Christ's sake, I delight in weaknesses, in insults, in hardships, in persecutions, in difficulties. For when I am weak, then I am strong" (2 Corinthians 12:9–10).

Perfectionism is one of the mightiest hope killers I know. But God removed the burden of perfection from you. Because of the grace of Christ on the cross, perfection is His job, not yours. God loves you just as you are. No perfection required.

When you're at your weakest, how do you draw strength from your relationship with Jesus Christ?

Cut out the Cut-Ins

You were running a good race. Who cut in on you …?
—GALATIANS 5:7

Do you ever look at the day's headlines and think, *What is this world coming to?* Well, that's what I thought about during my morning jog. I prefer to talk with God when jogging, but worries about the world kept cutting into my concentration.

God says we are all running our unique race, which means we all have good things to do. We can get sidelined by distractions, or we can continue strong. How? By doing all we can where we are—and praying about those things over which we have no influence.

What's the world coming to? I suspect that's not the real question. Perhaps we should be asking, *What's my run coming to?* Is it a directionless ramble, easily sidetracked, lacking purpose? Or is it focused, deliberate, and immune to "cut-ins"? I choose the second option. What about you?

What is trying to cut in on you: a gossipy friend, financial worries, too much reality TV, or something else?

A Story to Tell

Let the redeemed of the LORD tell their story—
those he redeemed from the hand of the foe.

—PSALM 107:2

God has given you an invaluable tool to use when embracing His opportunities. What tool? Your story. Yes, *your* story.

God will use your story, burdens and all, to build bridges, bind broken hearts, reveal Himself to people who need Him, and so much more.

He will use your story the moment you offer it up to Him, crude and incomplete as it may be. Long before you believe your story is ready for public consumption, God will be using "chunks" of it to bring hope and blessings to others. The story of your botched music audition at age twenty-two may be the only part of your story the woman sitting next to you in the airport needs to hear. It doesn't matter that you still have fourteen more years of story to tell. The moment you start this storying process is the moment you embrace opportunities from God.

What are you waiting for?

Lord, you are the author of my story. Show me how that story fits in with the greater story of your love for the world.

The Matterhorn's Message

Now all glory to God, who is able, through his mighty
power at work within us, to accomplish infinitely more
than we might ask or think.

—EPHESIANS 3:20 NLT

We had arrived at the most anticipated moment of our family trip in Europe: seeing the Matterhorn. Cloudy skies greeted us, but a Zermatt storeowner assured us the winds would eventually move the clouds. So we grabbed some hot chocolate and waited.

Sure enough, within an hour the Alps emerged. They were a sight to behold. Sort of. Our son Austin said what we were all thinking: "I expected more." We talked about life's build-ups and letdowns. Unnoticed by us, the clouds kept moving.

Suddenly Austin exclaimed, "Mom, Dad, what is that?" His smile said it all. What we had mistaken for the Matterhorn was only a small ridge of the Alps. Now, the true Matterhorn revealed itself, more spectacular than we could have imagined!

I believe God has a Matterhorn for each of us, an adventure with Him far better than we can imagine. My adventure began when I offered God all that I was—the good and the bad, my strengths and my weaknesses—so He could make me all He knows I *can be*.

What will you offer up to God today? His power will accomplish more than you can imagine.

Helpless Isn't Hopeless

The one who is in you is greater than t
he one who is in the world.

—1 JOHN 4:4

You know what makes me feel helpless? A flat tire. Or a box of metal pieces that are supposed to become a bicycle. But aren't we modern women able to handle anything?

As you've guessed, this is about more than flat tires and bicycles. Has anyone ever told you, "God will not give you more than you can handle"? Friend, let me tell you: Nowhere does God promise that life will not be more than we—Wonder Women that we are—can navigate. What He does say is that no matter what comes our way, He is in control. He can handle it.

Believe 1 John 4:4: God is greater than anything in this world, including whatever you are facing that is beyond your understanding or capacity. It's OK to feel helpless but don't give in to feeling hopeless.

God, you told us, through the apostle John, that your children overcomers, "because the one who is in [us] is greater than the one who is in the world" (1 John 4:4). Use this promise today to transform me from helpless to hopeful when things get tough.

Swap and Shop

We take captive every thought
to make it obedient to Christ.

—2 CORINTHIANS 10:5

Whe I was little, my parents listened to a radio program called *Swap & Shop*. People who were tired of their current belongings could call in and offer a swap so they could shop for something new.

Are you tired of your current thoughts? Swap them for something more uplifting. It works this way: when you think, for example, *I'm so afraid*, swap it with, *God has not given me a spirit of fear, but of a sound mind*. Get the idea?

For the next day, listen to your thoughts. Which ones do you want to swap? List them below or in your journal. Now, as you spend time in your Bible in the days ahead, "shop" for a Scripture to replace that old thought.

Condemnation-Free Zone

There is now no condemnation
for those who are in Christ Jesus.

—ROMANS 8:1

No condemnation? None? Zip? Zero? For me?

Yes, for believers it is true. When we feel another's disapproval, we can use this verse's truth to render powerless that person's judgment against us. They may condemn us, but God does not.

I'm learning, however, that as with most freedoms, freedom from condemnation carries great responsibility. You see, I can at times be severe in my thoughts toward people who've hurt or offended me. In those moments, I have a choice. I can unleash condemnation on that person, or I can remind myself that Christ freed me from all condemnation.

Give me grace today, Lord. I really want to let go of the hurt, to extend forgiveness, then move on condemnation-free. And I need your help. In your name, I pray. Amen.

The Lady in Gray

Encourage one another and build each other up,
just as in fact you are doing.

—1 THESSALONIANS 5:11

God often brings good from the bad in our lives by using other people. In my life it was someone I call "the lady in gray." She had lost her daughter in an accident, and I would see her at her daughter's grave. I would see the pain in her shoulders as she cried. And one day I dared to walk over and talk to her.

That conversation became one of my greatest blessings. Did you hear that? Even though she was in deep pain and grief, her burden became a blessing to me. At a time when I felt no one cared about me anymore, this grieving woman showed concern for me. The way she talked about Jesus gave me hope amid my hurt.

I never knew her name, and I've never seen her since. But I can't wait to meet her. So when you hear about a crazy woman running around heaven looking for a lady in a gray coat, that would be me! And I hope you'll come along, because I'd like to introduce her to you.

Who has been a "lady in gray" in your life? What did you learn from that person that you'd like to pass on to others?

The Best Seat in the House

Be renewed as you learn to know your Creator
and become like him.
—COLOSSIANS 3:10 NLT

Every time we choose to sit at Jesus' feet and worship, we experience a spa for the soul. When we leave a beauty spa, we are glowing from all those skin treatments. As we leave God's spa, we are glowing from being with Him. Our kids will notice it. Our coworkers will notice it. The people we connect with daily will notice it.

When we worship, the effect is the same as when we drop a dried-up sponge into a basin of water. We're transformed! The Greek word for "renewed" in Colossians 3:10 carries two connotations: (1) new strength and vigor and (2) changed into a new, better kind of life. And please don't overlook the path to that renewal: "know your Creator and become like him." How does that happen? Through sitting at His feet and focusing on reverencing and loving Him. That's worship.

All four Gospels give an account of a woman who kissed Jesus' feet, giving up her most precious possession in order to worship Him (Matthew 26:6–13; Mark 14:3–9; Luke 7:36–50; John 12:1–8). What did she give up? And what did Jesus say about her?

Spelling Lesson

We do not know what we ought to pray for,
but the Spirit himself intercedes for us
through wordless groans.
—ROMANS 8:26

A granddad overheard his granddaughter reciting the alphabet as she worked among their flowerbeds. He asked, "Whatcha doing?" The little girl answered, "I'm praying, but I can't think of exactly the right words. So I'm just saying all the letters. God will put them together for me, because He knows all the right words."

I love this story for its reminder that when we don't know what to think or say, we can continue praying and trusting in the one who knows. Let Him arrange the alphabet of your prayers.

If you'd like to have a little fun today, list the letters of the alphabet down the left side of a sheet of paper (or in your journal). Then next to those letters, write a word or phrase about God that starts with that letter. For example, A: Awesome, B: Beautiful, C: Caring, and so on.

Light in the Darkness

Your word is a lamp for my feet,
a light on my path.

—PSALM 119:105

At a point in my journey toward hope, when darkness seemed to be prevailing, I came upon this verse. I slowly grew to understand that God's truth shines light onto the path, but I have to choose to walk that path. I can't just stand there and admire it.

Does that sound daunting to you? Look at it this way: God could just point to the path and let you stumble along as best you can. But no, He not only prepared a path for you, but He prepared a light to guide you on that path. The light is His Word, your Bible.

Find hope today in the amazing gift of God's Word and in the Father's love behind the gift. Use a Bible concordance (either in print or online) to locate and write down at least six that contain the word hope.

Today Only

"Do not worry about tomorrow, for tomorrow will worry
about itself. Each day has enough trouble of its own."
—MATTHEW 6:34

In Exodus 16, we find the people of Israel in the wilderness
after Moses led them out of slavery in Egypt. They were less
than grateful for what God, through Moses, did for them.
They grumbled: "If only we had died by the Lord's hand in
Egypt! There we sat around pots of meat and ate all the food
we wanted, but you have brought us out into this desert to
starve" (v. 3).

Moses then spoke to the Lord on their behalf, and He
provided manna to feed them. Every morning it appeared,
and the people gathered whatever they needed for the day.
Their orders were to gather only one day's supply at a time.
If they gathered extra, the maggots got into it. This makes
sense in the days before Tupperware and refrigeration. But
something more is going on here than a lesson on food safety.
God was teaching His people to trust Him one day at a time
for their needs.

*God, help me to see your manna for me today, knowing that
tomorrow will have its own manna, for your supplies never
run low.*

Free to Ask

> "God, hear the prayers and petitions of your servant. …
> We do not make requests of you because we are righteous,
> but because of your great mercy."
>
> —DANIEL 9:17–18

Do you ever feel it would be selfish to ask God for His best? Do you ever think God must be too busy answering others' requests to be bothered with yours? Do you ever procrastinate in approaching God, thinking that when your life is more in order you will ask?

God promises to turn His ear toward us. The God of all heaven, the Creator of all things, He who breathes life into every soul, will hear and attend to your requests today.

If you could ask anything of God today, what would it be? Don't be afraid to ask. Your God is merciful. He has already granted you the freedom to come boldly before Him and seek His best. So ask! Then prepare to be amazed at what God does.

How has God answered your prayers so far this year? What prayer requests will you continue to bring before Him (either for yourself or on behalf of someone else)?

Redefining Slow

The Lord is not slow in keeping his promise.
—2 PETER 3:9

We live in a rush-rush, get-it-done-yesterday world. Even microwaves and drive-thru lanes are too slow for us sometimes. So when we read that God is not slow in keeping His promises, we think of that still unanswered prayer from six months ago, and we wonder. And discouragement creeps in.

Today, if doubt or discouragement nag at you, don't give in. Surrender instead to what you know to be true of God—that He is sovereign, that He is wise, that He is perfect in all ways, including in His timing. Choose today to shine with patient endurance and calm confidence that God's promises will be fulfilled. It's exactly what this hectic world needs to see.

Lord, you are not slow in keeping your promise; instead, you are patient, "not wanting anyone to perish, but everyone to come to repentance" (2 Peter 3:9). Give me the patience I need today to wait for your timing.

All Cleaned Up

Wash away all my iniquity
and cleanse me from my sin.
—PSALM 51:2

I loved cleaning up my boys when they were young. They'd come in from a day of playing outdoors, and they'd have that string of dirt beads around their necks as well as dirt under their little nails and between their toes. Dirt everywhere!

I didn't yell at them for having fun and getting messy. I was glad they'd had a good time. I just gathered them into the tub and applied soap and water and shampoo until all the dirt and grime was gone, and they were my fresh-smelling boys again.

That is how God sees us. Don't you think He knows we are going to get dirty as we live in this polluted old world? Your heavenly Father says to you, "Come on, little one, let's get you cleaned up again. Let's get you all shiny and looking your best." Then He cleanses away the shame and regret and sinful reactions and other "dirt" of the day until we glow again like daughters of the King.

Every night as you cleanse your face, ask God to cleanse your heart. Don't let the grime build up because you are ashamed or guilt ridden. Go to bed with thanksgiving in your heart because He has washed you and restored your glow.

February

Get Soaked

"Whoever drinks the water
I give them will never thirst."
—JOHN 4:14

Not too long ago I found a dried up sponge in my garage. It matched how I felt: sucked dry, brittle, used up. But when I dropped that sponge in water, it was restored to usefulness. As good as new.

Jesus promises in John 4:14 that something similar happens when we immerse ourselves in Him. Like living water, He fills us up, renews us, satisfies.

Has doing, doing, doing and working, working, working drained you of hope that you'll ever feel refreshed again? Make like a sponge and get wet! As you unload the dishwasher, praise God for one of His attributes with each glass, plate, fork you put away. Soak in the living water of worship.

Try one of these today: Pause to read a psalm. Listen to worship music as you make the kids' lunches. Sing to God in the car instead of muttering at the latest news.

Like Father, Like Child

Great are the works of the LORD; they are pondered
by all who delight in them.

—PSALM 111:2

I have long loved Psalm 112. It is my "go to" psalm when I'm tempted to give up, because it takes my eyes off the difficulty of living for the Lord and reminds me of the blessings. Read it, and I think you'll see what I mean.

But don't stop there. In fact, don't *start* there. Start with Psalm 111. The two belong together. One focuses on the deeds and character of the Lord Himself. The other focuses on the deeds and character of those who revere the Lord. As we take delight in the nature of God, our lives mirror His nature. Only because He is gracious and compassionate and generous can we ever expect to also be that way.

Our Lord's character and actions shape and guide our character and actions. That's the good news of these psalms when read together. We don't strive and exhaust ourselves to earn the blessing. The blessing is already promised for every child who delights in the company of her Father.

Just like the psalmist, I extol you, Lord, with my whole heart.
Great are your works and glorious are your deeds. Today
I put my trust in you; your righteousness will last forever
(Psalm 111:1–3).

Sticky Jesus

When they saw the courage of Peter and John
and realized that they were unschooled, ordinary men,
they were astonished and they took note that
these men had been with Jesus.

—ACTS 4:13

One Sunday, a pastor concluded his sermon by urging people to ask Jesus into their hearts. Afterward, a little boy ran to the front of the church.

"Pastor, you say I have to ask Jesus into my heart, right?"

The pastor said, "That's right."

"How big is Jesus?" the boy asked.

The pastor confirmed that Jesus was adult sized.

"That's what I thought," said the little boy. "So if I were to ask Him into me, wouldn't He stick out all over?"

That little boy had no idea how wise he was.

Every time I think of this story, I am challenged. And so I challenge you today: Wherever you go today, whomever you meet, whatever you say or do, don't be afraid to let Jesus stick out all over you.

True Beauty

Your beauty should not come from outward adornment,
such as elaborate hairstyles and the wearing of gold jewelry
or fine clothes. Rather, it should be that of your inner self,
the unfading beauty of a gentle and quiet spirit,
which is of great worth in God's sight.

—1 PETER 3:3–4

I love this quote from Audrey Hepburn: "For beautiful eyes, look for the good in others; for beautiful lips, speak only words of kindness; and for poise, walk with the knowledge that you are never alone."

If I were to make one tiny change, it might be to the last part: "walk with the knowledge *that you matter to God.*" But whether we quote my version or Audrey's, the message is clear: We can walk with poise and confidence because we know God is with us, and He is with us because He loves us.

Doesn't that make you feel beautiful today?

When others look at you today, what inner beauty do you hope they will see that might give them a glimpse of God?

The Eyes Have It

> "The LORD does not look at the things people look at.
> People look at the outward appearance,
> but the LORD looks at the heart."
>
> —1 SAMUEL 16:7

I'm still thinking of Audrey Hepburn's quote: "For beautiful eyes, look for the good in others."

Many of us spend a lot of time working on making our eyes as beautiful as possible. What we do with eye shadow, liner, mascara, brow pencils, and that ever-essential eye cream can make a big difference in our appearance. Aren't you thankful for eye makeup? I know I am!

But there's an even greater secret to beautiful eyes that many of us overlook. That secret is to look at people and things not through the world's lens, but through God's lens. With God's lens, we aren't swayed by outward appearance and trappings. Rather, we know that God's eyes look at the heart.

You see, we use our eyes to assign value. Let's assign value based on what's inside a person, not on what's outside.

Today look up the song "Beautiful for Me" by Nichole Nordeman and write down the lyrics that most touch your heart.

Fight for the Future

The weapons we fight with are not the weapons
of the world. On the contrary, they have divine
power to demolish strongholds.

—2 CORINTHIANS 10:4

Nothing can change your truth. I can't go back to when I
was four and change my life. I can't go back to being a
teenager either. I can't even go back to yesterday and erase
the mistakes I made. But that's not what God is calling us to
do.

The fight God we're in isn't the fight to change our past;
it's the fight to change our future. God wants to take the
words that have defined our pasts and put His truth on them.
We think our past will change the way God sees us, but God
doesn't see us any differently. He already knows us.

Every time we fight those damaging words—every time
we share a hurt—we are taking steps into a different future.
Every time we stand up to that thing that tells us we are mistakes, we step more into God's truth, and we see our burdens
transformed into blessings. And yes, there's always another
burden, but thank God there's also always another blessing.

*On a piece of paper, write down every hurtful and repulsive
thing that's been spoken about you. Then burn it, and prepare
to see God transform your burdens into blessings.*

Critic's Corner

I care very little if I am judged by you or by any human court; indeed, I do not even judge myself. My conscience is clear, but that does not make me innocent. It is the Lord who judges me.

—1 CORINTHIANS 4:3–4

One of my aunts always responded this way to news that she'd been criticized: "Well, honey, as long as they're talking about me, they're leaving someone else alone."

I'm not proud to admit this, but there have been times in my life when a single critical remark held the power to damage my self-image, make me question my worth, and stall my spiritual progress. God used my aunt's words to teach me two things: first, that to survive, we must learn how to cope with criticism; and second, survival does not mean we must give up on our desire to please. We do, however, have to rethink who we want to please.

The apostle Paul came under frequent and hurtful criticism. Yet he said he was not concerned about the judgments of others. He didn't even judge himself (wow!). Instead, he focused on pleasing the only one who really mattered, and that focus protected him from being derailed by critics.

What kind of impact might your life have once you learn how to handle criticism like Paul (and my aunt) did?

Our God Speaks

"New things I declare.
Before they spring into being I announce them to you."
—ISAIAH 42:9

This Scripture takes me back to that night as a four-year-old, removed from my home, petrified by the deep darkness of a strange bedroom. With not a glimmer of light to be seen, I felt I was about to be lost forever to darkness.

Many times in life I have felt such darkness. I couldn't figure out what God was doing or how He could bring anything good from my situation. Have you ever known that darkness—when you're lost in despair and confusion, perhaps because of your own foolish sin and mistakes, or when relationships break or a loved one dies or a medical diagnosis leaves you reeling? In these times, there seems to be no plan. Yet this Scripture is our hope. It assures us that God not only has a plan for us, but He also promises to reveal that plan.

Our God speaks!

Here's a faith builder for you: As you read through your Bible, pay attention to all the times and ways that God spoke. In Numbers 22, He once spoke through a donkey! This tells me that God will go to great lengths to communicate with you and me too. Thank Him for that today.

Seeing Eyes

Open my eyes that I may see wonderful things.
—PSALM 119:18

My husband, Lee, and I were returning home from my mother's funeral service. The storm outside our car fit the turmoil within me. Then Lee's voice broke through my wall of emotion. "Kim, open your eyes! You are not going to believe this!" His enthusiasm angered me. Couldn't he see I was grieving? Yet he persisted. "Kim, please, please, look up!"

Relenting, I opened my eyes. Dark skies had brightened, the thunder had silenced, the lightning halted. And stretched across the horizon was the most beautiful rainbow I'd ever seen.

I was immediately reminded of another rainbow given as a symbol of promise (Genesis 9:8–17). And in that moment, I knew I would find hope again. It took time and a lot of relapses, but as I focused little by little on the Source of hope, I found a life that exceeded anything I could have imagined.

Have you lost sight of hope? Don't despair. I speak from experience: Hope *will* return. But probably not in one mighty *whoosh*. More likely, it will return, as mine did, in tiny daily bits.

Lord, thank you for your patience with me when I focus on the storm instead of the rainbow. Today and each day, open my eyes to hope.

Can I Get a Witness?

Therefore, since we are surrounded by
such a great cloud of witnesses, ... let us run with
perseverance the race marked out for us.

—HEBREWS 12:1

The Bible is filled with stories from that "cloud of witnesses"—people who accomplished great things. One reason those stories are there, I believe, is to renew our hope when it falters. We are reminded that we too can become who God created us to be and accomplish what He wants us to do. I turn regularly to these stories so my hope can stay strong.

God designed us to be inspired by the lives of others. I believe you'll find great hope in reading about others who held on to hope in the direst of circumstances.

Set aside a few minutes today to read Hebrews 11. If you meet someone there whom you'd like to get to know better, use your Bible's index (or concordance) to seek out their fuller story.

What Good Is It?

Let us not become weary in doing good, for at the proper
time we will reap a harvest if we do not give up.

—GALATIANS 6:9

It's only normal to wonder if our lives are making a difference. Are the kids heeding our great advice? Are our tactful, nonthreatening ways of sharing our faith being noticed? Is God using anything we do to bring about anything good?

Sometimes I get spiritual obedience a bit confused with secular success. Secular success tends to be about big, noticeable results and basking in the attention they bring. But spiritual effort rarely brings instant gratification, and our individual contribution usually remains just a small, anonymous part of a much greater whole—and often invisible. If this is one of those days when you wonder if you are making a difference, let Galatians 6:9 welcome you to a new day filled with new ways to plant seeds!

As 1 Corinthians 3:6 describes it, one of us may plant a seed, someone else may come along and water, another may feed it, but ultimately it will be God who takes what we have done and makes it grow. Who has sown into your life, especially your walk with God? Whose life do you want to sow into?

Just Talk

> You know that the family of believers throughout
> the world is undergoing the same kind of sufferings.
> —1 PETER 5:9

Today's verse was written to early Christians who were being persecuted for their faith. But it contains a broader truth: we are not alone in our struggles. Our eyes may tell us everyone has it together except us, but we can't always rely on what we see. Honest dialogue—just talking—reveals what the eyes cannot: we are not the only ones dealing with fear, guilt, regret, pain, emotional suffering.

We need to break the silence, destroy our prisons of isolation, and begin honest dialogue with one another. Only then can our burdens transform into blessings.

Who can you call so you can discover together the power of "just talking"?

Things Kids Pray

"Ask and it will be given to you; seek and you will find;
knock and the door will be opened to you. For everyone
who asks receives; the one who seeks finds; and to the
one who knocks, the door will be opened."

—MATTHEW 7:7–8

When I had a severe gallbladder attack a few years ago, I said to my husband, Lee, "I wish a little child would pray for me." How does a child pray? She just says, "Dear God, please make Miss Kim better." And then off she goes, certain that God will take care of Miss Kim. How I wanted someone with that kind of belief to pray for me at that difficult time! How I want to learn to pray like that!

Lord, teach me to pray. Show me what to ask for. And give me endurance to keep asking, to keep seeking, to keep knocking … until my prayers are answered.

Lavish Love

See what great love the Father
has lavished on us.

—1 JOHN 3:1

"Jesus loves me, this I know." I used to sing those words while swinging on the front porch at night, serenading Daddy. Many times, I giggled in disbelief when Daddy told me that, as much as he loved me, there was someone who loved me even more. *No way*, I recall thinking. *How could that be?*

Now, as an adult, I know Daddy was right. He had planted truth in my heart: There is someone, Jesus, who does indeed love me more than anyone else can. And time and time again, when I've felt like a lonely little girl on a turbulent and terrifying journey, I have clung to that truth. Your Father's love is beyond any human love you can imagine. You cannot grasp it. You may doubt it, but that does not change the nature of His love. It is lavish, and it is yours.

In 1962, someone asked Swiss theologian Karl Barth how he would sum up his personal theology. He famously replied, "Jesus loves me, this I know, for the Bible tells me so." What would you say if asked the same question?

New Math

We have this treasure in jars of clay to show that
this all-surpassing power is from God and not from us.

—2 CORINTHIANS 4:7

All that I am is found in all that I am not. Does that sound like some strange new math to you? Let me explain.

Within myself I will never be whole. I will never be perfect. I will never be flawless. I will never have life all together. That's my on-my-own truth.

But here's my truth *with God*: After years of trying to hide who and what I *wasn't*, I realized I was hiding the best part of me. You see, Christ in me makes my brokenness beautiful. He perfects my imperfections, brings beauty to my flaws, and brings purpose and significance to what I had always declared a disaster. So now I delight in being a disaster, because with God, I'm a beautiful disaster!

Look up the group Hyland, whose song "Beauty in the Broken" describes the way God looks past our pain to see beauty in our brokenness.

What Does God Want?

He has shown you, O mortal, what is good. …
To act justly and to love mercy and to
walk humbly with your God.
—MICAH 6:8

We spend a lot of time wondering what God wants from us, don't we? People have done that since the beginning of time. In Micah 6, for instance, the Israelites were trying to figure out what they could bring to God to please Him (they knew their recent behavior hadn't been pleasing to Him at all). Verse 8 (above) answers the question. God wants His people to "act justly and to love mercy and to walk humbly."

"Act justly" means to live according to what we know is right and wrong.

In the Hebrew language, "love mercy" combines the concepts of loyal love and loving-kindness. Be kind to others, Micah is saying, and be loyal in your love for God, for He is loyal to you.

"Walk humbly" has little to do with our feet and a whole lot to do with our hearts. God wants us to depend on Him, not on our own abilities. He wants us to rely on His gift of forgiveness through His Son, not on our own perfect behavior.

What does God want from you? What pleases Him? Then pray you will love what He loves and value what He values.

It Came to Pass

In all this you greatly rejoice,
though now for a little while you may have
had to suffer grief in all kinds of trials.
—1 PETER 1:6

"It came to pass!" The entire room chuckled as the elderly woman proudly proclaimed her favorite Bible verse.

Thinking the old gal had misunderstood the question, the Bible study leader repeated the question she had asked: "What Bible verse has consistently gotten you through life's trials and temptations?"

The elderly woman replied, with even more emphasis, "It came to pass!" Seeing the mystified looks on the faces around her, she explained, "Well, it came to *pass* helped me remember that it didn't come to *stay*."

This lighthearted story contains a deep truth for each of us.

When a situation or person threatens your joy today, tell yourself, It came to pass.

Letting Grudges Go

Be completely humble and gentle; be patient,
bearing with one another in love.

—EPHESIANS 4:2

Are you the prisoner of a grudge? I've seen and experienced the destructive bondage of holding a grudge. I'm grateful that I've also witnessed the freedom that comes from looking into our "enemy's" eyes and asking ourselves, *What challenge is this person facing? Could he or she be carrying a great burden?*

Everyone we know carries wounds, hurts, and painful memories. When we keep that in mind, it's a little easier to treat one another more gently, to care instead of condemn, to love instead of loathe.

Freedom from grudge holding often begins with just talking. When we talk to each other, we begin to understand each other. When we understand, we begin to care. When we begin to care, we pray. When we pray for each other, we experience freedom to be honest, caring, and compassionate friends.

Loving Father, fill me with your gentle spirit today and free me from the grudges I'm holding against _____ (make it personal).

Wrong Question

But mark this:
There will be terrible times in the last days.
—2 TIMOTHY 3:1

Are we living in the last days? People ask me that question a lot, usually in response to shattering events like riots or earthquakes or epidemics.

I don't know the answer to that question. According to the Bible, God hasn't even given the answer to His own Son. If you hear a preacher proclaiming the date and time of the "last days," that preacher is claiming to know something Jesus doesn't know.

God's Word is full of answers for how to live wisely *every* day. Focus on applying that wisdom, and you'll be prepared for whatever may come next.

Ask yourself daily: What would I do differently today if I knew we were living in the last days?

That Inner Glow

Wisdom lights up a person's face.
—ECCLESIASTES 8:1 NLT

We go through a lot of money and effort to get our faces to glow. Yet the writer of Ecclesiastes offers a beauty secret we easily overlook: wisdom. As I've studied what the Bible has to say about true wisdom, I've created this easy-to-recall summary of how to acquire the GLOW of lasting inward beauty.

Gaze upward. We look for wisdom in all kinds of places, but true wisdom is found in God alone.

Look inward. As we seek God's wisdom in His Word, it shines a light on our hearts (not our husband's heart or coworker's heart but our own heart!). This look inward reminds us there is always room to grow.

Obey. Wisdom is active. When I know better, I want to do better. And God gives me power to be better, but I must take that next step. And the next. And the next.

Walk humbly with your God. A habit of gazing upward, looking inward, and obeying what God shows us to do leads to a lifelong walk of humility before God. Look at what God says: "These are the ones I look on with favor: those who are humble and contrite in spirit, and who tremble at my word" (Isaiah 66:2).

How can you get your GLOW on today? List some practical ways in your quiet time today.

Slaves to Statistics

It is for freedom that Christ has set us free.
Stand firm, then, and do not let yourselves
be burdened again by a yoke of slavery.

—GALATIANS 5:1

What do you need to be freed from today? Perhaps it's something you haven't even recognized as a form of slavery. When my mom died at age fifty-one of breast cancer, I felt I had been given a death sentence as well. I was in bondage to the fear of death. It took a lot of praying and studying Scripture for me to understand that my beginning date and ending date are not established by statistics, but by God alone. Sure, I do the responsible thing and have annual mammograms and physicals, and I hope you do the same. But Christ has freed me from my fear of death. And that freedom lets me hear from Him and serve Him daily, minus fear.

Ask your Father to show you any thought patterns and habits that are enslaving you today. He stands ready to set you free.

Not Just a Needle

> In Joppa there was a disciple named Tabitha
> (in Greek her name was Dorcas); she was always
> doing good and helping the poor.
> —ACTS 9:36

We don't know much about Dorcas, but she was important enough to be named in Acts. We know she was a disciple, someone who based how she lived on the teachings of Jesus.

In addition to being a disciple, she was "always doing good and helping the poor." Her good deeds included making clothing for the widows in her city.

I can imagine God looking at His faithful follower Dorcas, seeing a simple needle in her hand, and declaring, "I can work with that!"

I wonder if she had hoped to be chosen for so much more. Maybe she cried out silently, "I don't want a needle, I want a _____ (you fill in the blank)." If she did resist at first, she didn't resist for long. The Dorcas we see in Acts had surrendered what she already had—her needle—to the God who destines small things for perfect and profound purposes.

Today, numerous benevolent and charitable organizations have taken on Dorcas' name. Her legacy began with a needle in her hand. What is in your hand today?

Belly Praise

Praise the Lord, my soul; all my inmost being,
praise his holy name. Praise the Lord, my soul,
and forget not all his benefits.

—PSALM 103:1–2

Have you ever wondered what is in the very middle of the Bible? Well, this is it.

Praise. Praise from the poet king David's "inmost being."

The image here is of the whole belly. You've heard of belly laughs. Well, the middle verse of the Bible urges us to break out in some big old belly praise.

Is there a whole lot of praise going on in your "inmost being" today? If you need a praise prompt, read the rest of Psalm 103. You won't believe how many reasons you'll find there for letting loose with belly praise.

Heavenly Father, you forgive all my sins and heal all my diseases (v. 3). Thank you for redeeming my life from the pit and crowning me with your love and compassion (v. 4).

OK Is OK

Not that I have already obtained all this,
or have already arrived at my goal.
—PHILIPPIANS 3:12

Sometimes I feel very dissatisfied with myself. I'm a long way from where I want to be. It can overwhelm me at times. I'm learning, however, to fight that discouragement by letting Paul's words empower me.

In Philippians 3, Paul says his greatest desire is to know Christ and to be like Him. But he also acknowledges that he is far from where he wants to be (v. 12).

What I love about Paul is that no matter what he is feeling, he allows himself the freedom to feel it, and he also embraces the freedom to be real with those around him. I wonder if the key to his sense of freedom is knowing he also has the freedom to move beyond the stage in which he finds himself. He's not stuck. He's determined to press on (vv. 13–14). He's not going to give up. Don't you just love that!

Does the road feel long for you today? If so, then inhale deeply with a prayer, exhale with a new focus, and resolve to declare that it's OK. You may not be where you want to be, but, thank God, you are not where you used to be. And with that good news, press on!

Triple Promise

"Call to me and I will answer you and tell you great
and unsearchable things you do not know."

—JEREMIAH 33:3

God promises us that if we call on Him in prayer, He will
hear us, answer us, and tell us great and unsearchable
things we do not know.

How incredible that the God who spoke all things into
being loves you and me so much that He desires—yes,
desires—to communicate with us! I could rest in that truth all
day. How about you?

*Begin to keep a record of your prayer requests. When God
answers those requests, record those answers as well. That way
you will have a visible record of the truth of Jeremiah 33:3.*

Longing to Belong

"Follow me, and I will make you fishers of men."
—MATTHEW 4:19 RSV

Recently I overheard someone describe how defeated she felt because she hadn't been invited into the "right circle." She wondered why she wasn't making the desired impression on the people she wanted as friends. She speculated that there must be some unwritten criteria to be a part of the group.

I recall feeling the same way at times. No matter what age we reach, we all long for an invitation to join a circle of friends.

God knows our desire to be included, and He responds to our desire with His invitations to be a part of what He is doing in the world around us. We may feel a nudge to encourage a mom whose two-year-old is pitching a very public tantrum. We may feel a heart tug to text a friend. God extends to us all types of daily invitations to join Him and His circle.

And when we accept His invitation—even when it's not what we were hoping for—we experience the joy only He can give. God hears … God invites. We accept … we experience. Now, that's a great circle to be in!

In "Where I Belong" the lead singer of Building 429 describes how Jesus, not this world, is his true home. Check it out!

Impossible!

> By faith even Sarah, who was past childbearing age,
> was enabled to bear children because she considered
> him faithful who had made the promise.
>
> —HEBREWS 11:11

Would you have trouble believing the following advertisement?

"Over 100? Wife Barren? No Problem! Today You Can Conceive a Son."

God had promised Abraham a son, yet his wife, Sarah, was barren and laughed at the suggestion. Was her laugh caused by frustration, years of unfulfilled expectations, a "yeah right" kind of cynicism, anger, or mockery? We don't know. What we do know is what the writer of Hebrews tells us in the above verse: Abraham and Sarah's childlessness came to an end because Abraham believed God would be faithful to His promises. The circumstances hadn't changed: Sarah was still barren and Abraham was still old. But Abraham decided to put more faith in God than in his circumstances.

What is your "impossible" circumstance today? Tell God about it, and then, like Abraham, choose to put more faith in God than your circumstances.

In Reverse

"Come to me, all you who are weary and burdened,
and I will give you rest."
—MATTHEW 11:28

The Greek word for "rest" in this passage is *anapauo*, which means "to refresh by reversal." Jesus does not say bring your burden to Me so I can *erase* it—which He could do if He chose. Rather, He says bring your burden to Me so I can *reverse* it. Instead of negating all that you have survived, He wants to turn it around and give it purpose.

The Greek word for "burden" in this verse is *phortion*, and it means "a task or a service-in-waiting." Have you ever considered that the burden you are carrying is something God is waiting to use? Are you ready for your burden to be reversed from something that weighs you down and holds you back to something that frees you to be of service?

To you, your burden is useless. Worse than useless. As you spend time with God today, be honest with Him about how hard it is to imagine what good can come from your burden. But also thank Him for being more powerful, more creative, and more loving than you can imagine. Tell Him you trust Him to keep His promise to "reverse" your burden. Even trust the size of a mustard seed has power!

To Be Continued

And the God of all grace … will himself restore you
and make you strong, firm and steadfast.

—1 PETER 5:10

When Jesus told Peter he would disown Him, Peter declared, "Even if I have to die with you, I will never disown you" (Matthew 26:35). And then what happened? He disowned Jesus. Three times.

Peter loved Jesus, yet he let Jesus down. Like we love our friends and family but still let them down. That's our humanness. But it's what happens *after* Peter's failure that matters most to us today. Not long after His resurrection, Jesus approached His disciples on the shore (John 21). If I were Peter, I'd have wanted to hide. Wouldn't you? Yet Peter *ran* to Jesus. He was probably scared, certainly humbled, but he refused to hide from this teacher he loved but had let down.

Just then, Jesus must have loved Peter even more than ever. As He placed that nail-scarred hand on Peter's shoulder in welcome and acceptance, He spoke not a word of Peter's failure, just looked into his eyes and asked, "Peter, do you love me?" Then He gave Peter an assignment. "Take care of my sheep … feed my sheep." In other words, "Continue with your calling. It has not changed."

Thank Jesus for inviting you into His plans and purposes even though you sometimes falter and fail.

March

Focusing Forward

Forgetting what is behind and straining toward
what is ahead, I press on toward the goal.

—PHILIPPIANS 3:13–14

When I was young, I was sure Mother and Daddy had eyes in the back of their heads that gave them the ability to see what was going on behind them. As I grew up, I seemed to share that feature in that I was overly focused on what was behind me—my past. I saw only what had been and was not looking ahead. In addition, I viewed my past only from one perspective—my own—instead of seeking God's perspective. As a result, I could not make peace with my past; I could not let go of "what should have been." This backward focus blinded me to God's promises for my future.

No bad stuff from your past can keep God from doing great things in your life. So why focus on the past?

Ask God to open your eyes to what He's doing right now. Today. Then thank Him for being so much greater than your past.

Second Childhood

"Unless you change and become like little children,
you will never enter the kingdom of heaven."

—MATTHEW 18:3

These are puzzling words, aren't they? Why would Jesus want us to become like children? Children are needy, dependent, demanding little people. They cry when they feel like crying. They can't do a thing for themselves; they are so defenseless and vulnerable that they require constant caretaking.

They are embarrassingly honest. They haven't yet built up any resentment or prejudice. Their hearts harbor no hate. They … they … they … hmmmm. Are you starting to understand?

The world wants us to be strong and mature and unflappable and independent. But our Father wants us to come to Him with our needs, our vulnerability, our emotions—even the emotions that make us cry. May God help us be more childlike, so we can experience more of His perfect fathering.

Father God, grant me humility and show me how to become like a little child so I too can enter your kindgdom.

Sleep Aid

Yes, my soul, find rest in God;
my hope comes from him.
—PSALM 62:5

The moment I lie down to sleep, I begin to wrestle with to-morrow. Are you like that too? A multitude of "what ifs" haunt me. I rehearse the day's anticipated events and imagine every possible worst-case scenario.

The psalmist says, "Find rest in God." Maybe we should all carve those words in the headboards of our beds! Or maybe we should end each day by praying, "Good night, Lord. I leave tomorrow in Your sovereign hands." Many nights you won't want to pray those words. But keep praying them any-way. You'll enjoy more and better sleep. After all, tomorrow is already taken care of by God alone.

Find some peaceful praise and worship music to listen to as you fall asleep tonight. It's one way of observing this good bedtime advice: "Last word, God's Word."

Give It a Toss

Let us throw off everything that hinders.
—HEBREWS 12:1

When calling Lazarus from the dead, Jesus said, "Come out!" (John 11:43). He did not say, "Come out and run." He knew Lazarus' once-dead body would run again, just as He sees your running shoes lying there, waiting for the right moment. But first Lazarus had to be set free from the grave clothes that bound him. And we, too, have things we need to throw off each time we reach a new stage in our spiritual growth, and before the running can begin.

Make a list of what's hindering your progress right now. What is holding you back? Doubts? Worry? Do you feel unworthy? Is your life too busy? Maybe things have gotten so bad that you've concluded even God can't fix them. Maybe you face one big obstacle; maybe you face an assortment of little, annoying hindrances. Name them one by one. Then imagine standing on the edge of a cliff and throwing those hindrances over the edge, one by one. How good does that feel!

Dance Like a Squirrel

My God will meet all your needs according to
the riches of his glory in Christ Jesus.
—PHILIPPIANS 4:19

Have you ever watched squirrels dancing and prancing on tree limbs? The squirrels seem completely unaware of the danger that lurks if the tiny limb were to break. They are having too much fun as they dance around to worry.

Those squirrels are a great picture of how I view ministry. God calls us. We step out (perhaps on a shaky limb) and do what we can: plan, pray, pursue opportunities. He promises to supply all our needs according to His riches in heaven.

Yes, at times I worry about where the funds will come from to do what I believe God has called me to do. Yes, I sometimes worry that no one will show up for a women's retreat or other event where I'm teaching. But I'm dancing on the fact that if what I am doing is truly God's will, the limb will not break. The invisible Hand that holds my ministry will also be the Hand that touches hearts to support it with their finances or participation.

Are you dancing on a limb of some sort today? Take a lesson from a squirrel. Dance like you know who holds that limb.

Conversing with God

The LORD would speak to Moses face to face,
as one speaks to a friend.

—EXODUS 33:11

Friendships thrive when we allow time simply to talk. Your time to talk with God might be while preparing dinner or riding the subway to work or folding the laundry—or all of the above. I use my daily runs to talk with God. I share whatever is on my mind—what I'm happy about, what confuses me, what I think I need. I ask God lots of questions—He can handle it. I'm as real with God as I know how to be. That's the way it should be between friends.

A friendship with God also thrives when we take time to listen. I want to know what God thinks. Midway through most of my jogs, I shift from talking to God to listening to God. If I hear from God during my jog, I quickly write down what He impressed upon me once I get home.

Carve out a little talk-and-listen time from your schedule today. Give God your undivided attention, even if just for a few minutes. He's a wonderful conversationalist!

Hand in Hand

"I, the LORD ... will take hold of your hand."
—ISAIAH 42:6

Among my favorite childhood memories are my walks with Daddy. My little arm could barely reach and hold on to the big hand he extended to me. But the security, the sense of belonging, the pure joy it brought kept me holding on long after my arm had fallen numb. That's the image that comes to my mind as I read today's passage. And with God, I don't have to hold on because His hand is holding on to me.

Let one of your own childhood memories be a starting place for your belief in God's love for you to grow. I say "starting place" because God's love so surpasses even the best human love that no earthbound memory or longing can quite capture it. Your Father wants to love on you even more than you want to be loved.

Do you have a memory of a time when you felt thoroughly loved and secure? If so, take some time to write about it today. If not, tell God about your longing for this kind of love.

What Language Is That?

Gracious words are a honeycomb,
sweet to the soul and healing to the bones.

—PROVERBS 16:24

Some of our little neighbors, ranging in age from three to ten, were visiting one day, and I pulled together a craft project for us to do. Amid all the energetic cutting and pasting, the fussing began. "I can't do this right." "I can't get it straight." "This is too hard." "I don't think I like this."

I was trying to think of a way to wrap up the activity and move us on to something new when a few apt words broke through the rising frustration. The littlest child of all, his finger pointed for emphasis, asked, "So girls, what am I hearing? Am I hearing Chinese, Japanese, or a little Whine-ese? Oh, I know, I'm hearing some Whine-ese!"

Everyone chuckled, and fun returned to our activity.

Many times since that day I have used this little boy's words to ask myself, *What language am I speaking? Am I speaking Whine-ese and creating frustration and tension?* If so, I can shift the atmosphere just as quickly as my little friend did by remembering to keep my words sweet and healing!

Sweeten my speech today, Lord, with your grace, so my words will bring healing to the hurting.

Perfect Timing

There is a time for everything,
and a season for every activity under the heavens.

—ECCLESIASTES 3:1

While visiting my son at college some years ago, I could see he was disheartened by his failure to earn a starting position on the football team as a freshman. Understanding his feelings, his coach looked at me and said, "Your son has great potential. He is going to have a great career. But for now, he is right where he needs to be."

May I pass along to you that godly coach's encouragement and hope? You are right where you need to be. If like my son, you are feeling sidelined, let me assure you: You have not been forgotten or overlooked. Your Coach sees your fears and frustrations, and He knows your potential. He has brought you to this moment, and you are right where you need to be.

Sometimes God moves faster than we want. At other times, He seems to take forever. The truth is, God's timing is always perfect.

Take some time out of your busy day to thank God that He's got you right where you need to be in this moment.

The Designer's Touch

Have you not heard? The LORD is the everlasting God,
the Creator of the ends of the earth.

—ISAIAH 40:28

When my window treatments arrived, my excitement soon gave way to frustration because I could not arrange the different sections to make them match the picture. Finally I gave up and called the seamstress. As soon as she arrived, she effortlessly flicked the fabric into place.

"How in the world did you do that?" I asked. Her answer was profound: "I designed them." Then she added, smiling, "You should have called me first, because even when you make a mess of them, I know exactly how to put them back as they should be."

When life becomes twisted and tangled, I think we sometimes believe God is as befuddled as we are. In truth, with a mere flick of His hand, He sets kings on thrones and removes them; He heals tumors, restores incomes, and mends marriages.

No matter what is happening in my life—and no matter how hard I struggle and strive and work to set things right—in the end I have to call upon my Creator and Designer.

What are you facing today? Whatever it is, stop for a moment to call on your Heavenly Designer for help with the messes life inevitably brings.

What Will They Think?

Anxiety weighs down the heart,
but a kind word cheers it up.

—PROVERBS 12:25

One of the greatest hindrances to our spiritual health is the refrain "What will they think?" And "they" is not "the world." Our perceived threat of rejection comes from those who sit with us in church and in Bible study, those we call friends.

I recall the day (more than twenty years ago) I first shared with a group of my friends some issues I was sure would send them running. Though I may have appeared "together" as their ministry leader, I was about to expose my secret pain of anorexia, anxiety attacks, and more. And this is what I learned: My friends cared *more* deeply for me after I shared. The things I had tried so desperately to keep hidden were the very things God used to give my friends freedom to share *their* fears and worries.

On a popular TV show, one depressed person looked at the other and said, "We should have been talking." This is the message for today: We should be talking!

What scares you most about sharing your burdens with another person? Ask God whom He wants you to talk with. Will you run toward that opportunity?

Power for Patience

> We continually ask God to fill you with the
> knowledge of his will ... being strengthened with
> all power according to his glorious might so that you
> may have great endurance and patience.
>
> —COLOSSIANS 1:9, 11

When I came across the "so that" in Colossians 1:11, I hoped to read I would be strengthened *so that* I could accomplish great things today or be freed from all my worries. Maybe you'd like to be strengthened, so you don't snap at your kids. Or so you can resist that extra helping of pie or remain gracious toward your coworkers.

But that's not what Paul had in mind. He prays we will be strengthened *so that* we may have great endurance and patience. OK, I know endurance and patience are good things—but really, they've rarely been my goals. I'd rather be victorious than to endure. And patience? You can count me among the friends of the writer of Psalm 6:3 who asked, "How long, Lord, how long?"

Asking for endurance and patience is not the grand ending I wanted from Paul's prayer, but you, God, know that long-suffering is a greater gift than quick and easy results. Fill me with the knowledge of you, instead of showy victories that make me look good but do nothing to take me deeper with you.

Oh Mercy!

"Be merciful, just as your Father is merciful."
—LUKE 6:36

A friend of mine described this experience: "Yesterday a cashier rang up my purchase wrong. I was already in my car when it occurred to me that I had paid a lot more than I expected, and so I checked my receipt. I went back in the store and waited in a long, slow line to speak to the same cashier. I was in a hurry and on the edge of irritable.

"When it was my turn, the cashier recognized me and looked scared. That got to me. My attitude changed instantly from mean to merciful. I smiled, joked about being back again already, and then I told her what had happened. She started apologizing frantically. Turns out it was her first week on the job. I reassured her that anyone could have made the same mistake, I wasn't upset, and I bet I'd make way more mistakes if I had her job. By God's grace, I didn't make her feel stupid. I did not make her feel shame for inconveniencing me. I chose to let God take over and flow mercy to her."

In what ways can you be more merciful today? Maybe an act of kindness, a refusal to belittle or retaliate, will be the closest someone comes to seeing God today.

Never Abandoned

"He calls his own sheep by name."

—JOHN 10:3

God sees you today. He knows you personally and intimately. From among any crowd, He can pick you out and call you by name.

How can you be sure of this? Because the Good Shepherd described in today's verse is also your heavenly Father who created you, loves you, and knows the real you. If you are feeling misplaced at work, or reeling from an argument that has left you isolated, or feeling abandoned because your prayers remain unanswered, be assured: You are not forgotten. Your Shepherd sees you. He whispers, "Just stay still. I know exactly where you are, and I'm on my way to get you."

You may feel forgotten at times, but you never are.

Do you know someone who needs to hear this message? Pass it on.

Stay Wet!

"If you knew the gift of God and who it is that asks
you for a drink, you would have asked him and he
would have given you living water."

—JOHN 14:10

A dried-up sponge is renewed almost instantly when placed in a basin of water. But once it is removed from water, a sponge begins to dry out again. Little by little, all that water leaks away or evaporates, and what's left is something hard, flat, and unrecognizable.

We're not very different from sponges. That's why Jesus said, "*Remain* in me" (John 15:5). We don't stay renewed by remaining in a basin of water (or even a lovely bubble bath); we remain in Jesus, the same Jesus who once told a Samaritan woman that He was "living water" (see John 14:7–14).

Remaining is all about relationship—*my* relationship with Jesus. No one else can do it on my behalf. I cannot rely on other people's relationship with Christ to pump me up. When Jesus invites us to remain in Him, He invites us by name. No one else can accept that invitation for us.

How will you respond today to Jesus' invitation to receive living water?

Fruit Bearing

"You did not choose me, but I chose you and appointed you
so that you might go and bear fruit—fruit that will last."

—JOHN 15:16

When we remain in Christ, we receive a promise. "I will remain in you" (John 15:4). Through thick and thin, happy and sad, busyness and boredom, failures and triumphs, He will always remain in us. And as He remains in us, He will transform us into what He calls a fruit bearer. We will discover, for instance, that by remaining in Christ, we start to take on some of His qualities like love, joy, peace, patience, kindness, goodness, faithfulness, gentleness, and self-control (see Galatians 5:22–23). I can assure you as one who has tried: Those qualities cannot become part of us in any lasting way by self-effort; they can only come from Christ remaining in us.

Read chapter 15 of John's Gospel, then write down the imagery for Jesus that you find there.

Don't Push Me

The LORD upholds all who fall and lifts up those who are
bowed down.

—PSALM 145:14

You may have noticed by now that I love jokes. I especially enjoy the ones that cause us to pause and recognize some of our off-kilter ideas about ourselves and our God. Here's one of those for today.

A little girl, dressed in her Sunday best, was late and running to her Sunday school class. As she ran, she prayed, "Dear God, please don't let me be late. Dear God, please don't let me be late." Then she fell.

She got up, dusted herself off, and saw that her dress was now dirty and had a little tear. She started running again, still praying, "Dear God, please don't let me be late." But this time she added, "But please don't push me, either!"

Think about a time when you were humbled or "fell" in the figurative sense. How did God uphold you and lift you up?

Temporary Status

God sets the lonely in families.
—PSALM 68:6

I was leaving friends, church, and routine, and closing the doors of my national women's ministry. I was taking my boys from a home and life they loved. It was more than I thought this mom's heart could endure. But we trudged ahead.

Within days of our arrival in our new town, I was at the batting cages watching my guys go on with life. They had fears and uncertainties, of course, but they kept going. By day's end, they had made a new friend, a boy who had lost his family at a very young age and grown up without the simplest of things, like birthday celebrations.

That moment initiated a shift in my perspective about our move. And it introduced my family to someone who, to this day, remains very special in our lives.

Wherever you live, you're a temporary resident. But your temporary residencies will be filled with opportunities of eternal outcome.

Fighting against where you are only distracts you from seeing that you have been placed for a purpose. Sit still for a bit and ask God what He wants you to do today—right where you are, even if it isn't where you want to be. There could be a blessing in store. (I speak from experience!)

Trust and Obey

Trust in the LORD with all your heart, and lean not on
your own understanding; in all your ways submit to him.
—PROVERBS 3:5–6

Let's travel to the shores of the Sea of Galilee to sit among
some five thousand men, along with the women and children. Jesus had just finished speaking, and the sun was beginning to set.

Toward evening the disciples approached him. "We're
out in the country and it's getting late. Dismiss the people so they can go to the villages and get some supper."

But Jesus said, "There is no need to dismiss them.
You give them supper."

"All we have are five loaves of bread and two fish,"
they said.

Jesus said, "Bring them here." (MATTHEW 14:15–18 MSG)

Whatever the disciples thought, they chose to do exactly
what He asked. And because of their obedience, they became
participants in one of the most talked about and beloved miracles of the Bible.

*Isn't this what you desire? To be a part of something so much
bigger than what you alone can accomplish? If so, write out
Proverbs 3:5–6 on an index card or sticky note, put it somewhere
noticeable, then allow the words to sink into your heart and mind.*

Good Choice

"As for me and my household,
we will serve the Lord."

—JOSHUA 24:15

God did not make us robots. When He created us, He empowered us to make our own choices.

When Joshua spoke his rousing words to the Israelites, they were at an important crossroads. They had left behind Egypt and the wilderness to cross the Jordan River into the Promised Land. And now in the Promised Land, they were surrounded by pagan people who worshiped strange new gods. Would they long for the Egyptian gods they left behind? Would they be seduced by the new gods they were hearing about? Listen again to what Joshua said to the people in this dramatic moment: "If you decide that it's a bad thing to worship GOD, then choose a god you'd rather serve—and do it today. Choose one of the gods your ancestors worshiped from the country beyond The River, or one of the gods of the Amorites, on whose land you're now living. *As for me and my family, we'll worship God*" (Joshua 24:15 MSG, emphasis mine).

We face choices each day. Combined, our choices answer an important question: Who will we serve today?

Pray for God's help to resist serving unworthy gods today and to stay focused on choosing what will bring Him glory.

Bankable Truths

> I am convinced that neither death nor life,
> neither angels nor demons, neither the present
> nor the future, ... nor anything else in all creation,
> will be able to separate us from the love of God.
>
> —ROMANS 8:38–39

Suppose I handed you a new $100 bill. Wouldn't you think, *Oh my, just imagine what I can do with that!* What if I crumpled it right before your eyes? What if I threw the bill on the ground and stomped on it? If you're like me, you'd still want it, because a beat-up $100 bill is still worth a hundred dollars.

Now consider what God sees today as He looks at you. He sees that you've been scuffed by life's disappointments and challenges. He sees your struggle with hurtful voices of the past. Yet He beckons you to continue your journey with confidence that you are loved. That you are His chosen child. That today holds not just any plan, but *your* plan—a worthy, significant plan. And that absolutely nothing can devalue you or take from you what God has given.

Find your quiet place where you can listen. Do you hear your Creator as He declares, smiling: Oh my, just imagine what I am about to do with you today! Tell Him much you look forward to spending your day in His company.

Wounded Healers

He was pierced for our transgressions, he was crushed
for our iniquities; the punishment that brought us peace
was on him, and by his wounds we are healed.

—ISAIAH 53:5

Are you feeling too wounded to be of any help to anyone
else? Listen to these words from the late Henri Nouwen,
from his book *The Wounded Healer*:

"Nobody escapes being wounded. We all are wounded
people, whether physically, emotionally, mentally, or spiritually. The main question is not 'How can we hide our wounds?'
so we don't have to be embarrassed, but 'How can we put
our woundedness in the service of others?' When our wounds
cease to be a source of shame, and become a source of healing, we have become wounded healers."

*Do these seem like positive or negative words for you? Pause
today to tell God how you feel about embracing the role of
wounded healer as part of His unfolding plan for you.*

Historically Correct

"I, even I, am he who blots out your transgressions,
for my own sake, and remembers your sins no more."
—ISAIAH 43:25

Do you ever get historical with your spouse? Your children? Notice that I did not say "hysterical." I said *historical*. When we are upset, we bring up everything that person has ever done to annoy us. That's getting historical.

The good news is, God never does that to His children. He doesn't bring up what He has already forgiven. He chooses not to remember our sin. He chooses, instead, to remember the cross, where He asked His only Son to suffer and die in our place for our sins.

The next time you start to get historical with someone, remember the cross. That's the history that matters most.

Reflect on ways you may have hurt others, asking the Holy Spirit to reveal this to you. After asking God for forgiveness, prayerfully consider whether you need to make amends to those you hurt, either by writing a letter or initiating a heart-to-heart conversation.

To Die For

> "For God so loved the world that he gave his one
> and only Son, that whoever believes in him shall
> not perish but have eternal life."
> —JOHN 3:16

Today I came across the saying, "I may not be perfect, but Jesus thinks I'm to die for."

Let that sink in for a moment. Do you see the shift in focus? Most of us focus on our imperfections. On how far we still have to go to "measure up." What if we focus instead on the already Perfect One who looks at you and me today, just as we are, and finds us lovable, acceptable, and worth dying for?

Did you get that message? Jesus looked across the expanse of time, He saw you as you are this very minute, and He whispered, "You, I choose. You, I love."

For a first step toward this new focus, I invite you to memorize John 3:16 (above). Then personalize it: "God so loved me, Kim (substitute your first name), that he gave his one and only Son, that if I believe in him I will not perish but have eternal life."

Cross Purposes

And God is able to bless you abundantly, so that
in all things at all times, having all that you need,
you will abound in every good work.
—2 CORINTHIANS 9:8

Every time I see a cross, I am reminded of the cost that was paid in full to ensure my eternal security. But that is not all the cross means to me. It is also my daily assurance that Christ is on my side, and He is working on my behalf. It is my reminder that even when life is full of hurt, I can keep moving forward in hope and power to serve others.

In the midst of whatever is going on in your life, how are you serving the one who loves you so? Do not be defeated by your circumstances. Choose instead to praise Jesus even if you feel like you're wearing a crown of thorns. Dare to rise up out of that pit of anger and walk out of that prison of the past. What seems like your crown of thorns can also reflect God's love!

Show me, God, someone I can serve today, knowing that the Christ of the cross is now by my side. May I spread your love to those who need it the most.

Hunger Pains

"Blessed are those who hunger and thirst for righteousness,
for they will be filled."

—MATTHEW 5:6

Have you ever gossiped, lost your temper, or lied to get out of an awkward situation? Did it eat at you afterwards? I believe that's a sign you are hungering and thirsting for righteousness. At one time, you may not have thought twice about such behavior. But now you know the cost Jesus paid on the cross to cover sins like anger and envy and dishonesty. You know what it cost Him, and you love Him for it, and you long to demonstrate that love by living in a way that honors Him.

When you hear a news story about cruelty or depravity and you find yourself longing for this world to be better, that too is your hunger and thirst for righteousness. Don't despair—of yourself or the world you live in. You will be filled—that's the blessing Jesus offers to hungry, thirsty people like you. His power at work within you will transform you, little by little, so that your family resemblance to Him will grow ever more striking. Those aren't just hunger pains; they are also growing pains.

How has this devotional changed your perspective on what it means to hunger and thirst for righteousness?

An Audience of One

Moses raised his arm and struck the rock twice
with his staff. Water gushed out, and the community
and their livestock drank.

—NUMBERS 20:11

It's a miracle! Water flowed from a rock! The people were jubilant. Moses was a success.

Well, Moses was successful in the eyes of the people, but in God's eyes—not so much. God told Moses to speak to the rock, but Moses struck the rock with his rod. We can speculate on why Moses did what he did, but God summed it up this way: "You did not trust in me enough to honor me as holy in the sight of the Israelites" (v. 12).

As we use our gifts and talents, we may be able to make those around us *oooh* and *ahhh*. But let's not confuse the applause of others with the will of God. Let's make sure all the glory goes to the Giver of our influence, skill, and giftedness.

*Lord, it's so easy sometimes to get wrapped up in being
successful for you instead of obedient to you. Help me walk
through this day with a focus on your glory, not mine.*

Pass the Wisdom, Please

Walk with the wise and become wise,
for a companion of fools suffers harm.

—PROVERBS 13:20

Nothing complicated about today's verse. *You grow in wisdom as you hang out with wise people.* You may not always be comfortable with these people: Wise people are truth tellers, and sometimes the truth can hurt. But the benefits far outweigh the momentary discomfort.

Who are the wise people in your circle of acquaintances? Who would you like to "walk with" more regularly so that his or her wisdom rubs off on you? You see, there's something else that wise people do: They share the wisdom they have acquired. Paul describes the process in 2 Timothy 2:2: "The things you have heard me say in the presence of many witnesses entrust to reliable people who will also be qualified to teach others." Who's qualified? The wise. So find that wise guy or gal and insist they pass it on.

Make a date to get lunch or coffee in the coming week with that wise person you identified.

Heart Hurt

I pour out before him my complaint;
before him I tell my trouble.
—PSALM 142:2

When the boys were little, I was good at was noticing when they were hurting. But little boys don't talk about such things. So I learned to wait. After dinner was done, I would call out to Trey or Austin, "Come sit with Mommy for a while." And we would talk about this and that, but eventually I'd get to the question I really wanted to ask: "What hurts your heart?"

And the words spilled out of those boys. One time Austin told me, "Mommy, it really hurts my heart that you won't let me dye my hair orange!" Another time he said, "Mommy, it really hurts my heart that Daddy won't let me have my ear pierced." He was four years old.

But my favorite is when he said, "Mommy, it really hurts my heart when you won't let me sleep with you and Daddy every night!" I said, "Austin, you don't understand, but it really hurts Daddy's heart when I let you sleep with us every night!"

Sometimes I could make everything OK again during our talks. But most important was us being able to talk and walk in step with one another.

What kind of communication do you think your heavenly Father would like with you?

Spring Cleaning

Let us stop passing judgment on one another.
—ROMANS 14:13

The story is told of a young couple who worked hard, saved money, and finally found their dream home. Shortly after moving in, the couple sat at their kitchen table one morning, eating breakfast. The wife looked out the window and, to her surprise, saw her neighbor hanging dirty laundry on the clothesline.

"That laundry isn't clean!" she told her husband. "She needs to learn a thing or two about washing her clothes!"

A few days later, as the couple sat at their kitchen table for another meal, the wife again noticed her neighbor hanging laundry on the clothesline. This time something was different.

"Wow!" she said to her husband. "Her clothes are really clean! Someone must have taught her how to do laundry properly!" Without raising his head from his plate, the husband gently responded, "Actually, honey, I got up early this morning and washed the window."

And so it is with life. What we see when watching others depends on the window through which we look. Washing our own windows from time to time changes our perspective.

When have you passed judgment on someone, maybe even without knowing it?

April

Dressed for God's Best

Put on the full armor of God, so that you can
take your stand against the devil's schemes.

—EPHESIANS 6:11

We gals can spend a lot of time deciding what to wear, can't we? Is it seasonal? Is it age appropriate? Is it fashionable? Fun? In the summer, we ask, "Is it cool?" In frigid weather, the key question is often, "Is it warm?" Protection can be more important than prettiness at times.

Have you ever taken a close look at the God-designed outfit described in Ephesians 6:11–17? God designed these items of clothing for far more than protection against the weather. They help us conquer the daily attacks and temptations that come our way. I love that this attire is always in season, is one-size-fits-all, and … is free.

But what I love most is what this attire reveals about God's thoughtfulness and care toward us. Just as we take time choosing our daily attire, He took time thinking of how He could best protect us so we could live confidently and walk courageously into the plan He has for us.

Get acquainted with the six pieces of God-designed armor in Ephesians 6 by listing each item. Now you know how to dress for God's best.

What's on Your Belt?

Stand firm then, with the belt of truth
buckled around your waist.
—EPHESIANS 6:14

Among a first-century Roman soldier's gear was a broad leather belt that kept everything in place and at hand for battle. Special hooks and holders secured a sword or quiver at the proper angle and held supplies of bread, oil, and water. The belt included an apparatus on which to rest a battle shield, and clips to hold the breastplate in place, leaving a soldier's arms free to wield a sword, fling a rock, or let fly an arrow.

Like those soldiers, I find that the truths (or lies) I hang on my belt each day make all the difference in whether I walk in freedom or in fear.

Jesus said, "Then you will know the truth, and the truth will set you free" (John 8:32). What truths will you clip to your belt today, so you can walk in freedom instead of fear?

Shameless

Stand firm ... with the breastplate
of righteousness in place.
—EPHESIANS 6:14

No Roman soldier would go into battle without his breast-plate. This sleeveless piece covered the torso to protect the heart and other major organs, including the intestines. In New Testament times, the heart symbolized the mind and will, and the bowels symbolized the seat of emotions. And when you think about it, that's where we are most often attacked, isn't it? Our minds and emotions.

When the bills aren't getting paid, or a hurtful relationship can't be reconciled, or our bodies weaken from illness, the lies chime in. *You're nothing special*, they whisper. *Things aren't going to work out for good. God is very, very unhappy with you.* The lies will win the battle ... unless we are clothed with our breastplate of righteousness.

The word *righteousness* declares that we are in "right standing with God." In legal terms, we have been found "not guilty." In emotional terms, we've been set free from the shame of inadequacy and worthlessness that plagues us. In spite of all our shortcomings, failures, and dysfunction, God has put His stamp of approval on us.

Walk through your day in the freedom of knowing you are A-OK with God.

Killer Shoes

Stand therefore, ... having shod your feet with
the preparation of the gospel of peace.
—EPHESIANS 6:14–15 NKJV

We all love shoes, right? Well, let me tell you, if you had seen the shoes of the typical Roman soldier in the first century, you would have seen some *real* killer shoes. Made of heavy metal and leather, they were covered with sharp spikes.

It's ironic that Paul would connect these warlike shoes with peace. But when he wrote the above words, I believe he was thinking about how those no-nonsense shoes held the Roman soldiers in place. You see, some of those spikes were on the soles of the shoes. When the enemy attacked, the well-shod soldiers dug in their spikes and stood firm, immoveable.

Does it feel like life is pushing you around? Put on your killer shoes that equip you to stand firm. When you're able to stand firm, you feel secure, right? You feel at peace about your circumstances. And this peace gives you the assurance you need to step out in faith and in step with God.

The next time someone tells you, "Those are killer shoes you're wearing!" think about your feet as being "shod ... with the preparation of the gospel of peace" (v. 15).

Soak Your Shield

Take up the shield of faith, with which you can
extinguish all the flaming arrows of the evil one.

—EPHESIANS 6:16

Have you ever been going about your day when a random
thought pierces your mind and leaves you unable to think
of anything else? Paul calls these invasive thoughts "flaming
arrows." They have the power to render us useless and hopeless.

But Paul tells us how to protect ourselves: the shield of faith.

In New Testament times, the tips of long, slender arrows
were wrapped with fabric soaked in flammable fluids. Their
hollow interiors were also filled with flammable fluids that
exploded upon impact. To protect themselves, Roman soldiers had to plan ahead. They had to soak their shields in
water so that, when battle erupted, the fiery darts were ren-
dered harmless.

God has given us our own shield of faith. How do we use
it? Romans 10:17 (NKJV) tells us that "faith comes by hearing, and hearing by the word of God." As we soak ourselves
in God's Word and, by faith, accept His Word as truth, it
becomes our shield, deflecting life's flaming arrows and extin-
guishing their power.

*Before you leave home today, take a few minutes to soak up
some of God's truths. Then, with your shield of faith in place,
you're good to go!*

Sixty Thousand Thoughts

Take the helmet of salvation and the sword of the Spirit,
which is the word of God.

—EPHESIANS 6:17

According to the National Science Foundation, our brains produce as many as sixty thousand thoughts per day. The report goes on to say that the majority of these thoughts are nonsense. We dwell on the past or the future. We worry. We drift into fantasy, fiction, and negativity.

That's why our minds need protection. We need a helmet, and not just any helmet. The helmet of *salvation*. Protection begins with Christ. *He* is our salvation.

How does Jesus protect our minds? He invites us into a relationship with Him. If we accept His invitation, we get to know Him and experience His presence with us. Over time, we begin to think like He thinks. We start to align our thoughts to His thoughts.

So some of our thinking is transformed as we let Jesus "rub off" on us. But some of it requires effort and choices on *our* part. This is what the Bible means when it says to "take captive every thought to make it obedient to Christ" (2 Corinthians 10:5).

When can you spend time with Christ today, so His thoughts become your thoughts?

Keep Swinging

Take ... the sword of the Spirit, which is the word of God.

—EPHESIANS 6:17

Because of His great love for us, God has given us everything we need—a complete wardrobe—not only to get over the hurts and burdens we bear but to make good use of them. And one piece of that wardrobe is a sword—the Word of God. The Bible describes our sword as living and active and sharp (Hebrews 4:12).

When your mind says, *I can't do this anymore*, your sword cuts quickly through that lie with God's truth: "I can do all things through Christ" (Philippians 4:13 NKJV).

When your mind says, *I give up; it's too late*, your sword delivers a fatal blow to that lie: Don't grow weary; at just the right time your reward will come (Galatians 6:9).

When fear grips your soul, one swing of your sword can expel the fear with the reminder that God has not given you a spirit of fear (2 Timothy 1:7).

When the fiery darts declare, *Your life is a mess*, your sword exposes the truth that God can take everything in your life and make it work for your good and His glory (Romans 8:28).

Memorize one of the Scriptures in today's devotional. A single swing of your powerful sword can make a huge difference.

An Amazing Story

"It was not you who sent me here, but God."
—GENESIS 45:8

The life of Joseph (Genesis 30–50) is a story of extreme highs and extreme lows that took him from the pit to the prison to the palace. I can see God at work from the story's beginning until its final chapter. But I doubt Joseph found his life as amazing as he lived it from day to day, wondering what was going to happen next. One day honored by his father; the next day sold into slavery by his brothers. One day promoted and the next day punished for doing the right thing.

We all have moments when we wonder what is going on. We cannot see the next chapter in our story, but we can choose to believe God is working for our good whether we're in the pit or the palace. One day our children, or their children, or those who knew us best will look back at the story we left behind and be amazed—because they will be able to see how God was at work all along, accomplishing a greater outcome than anyone dared to imagine.

Tell God about a situation that feels like a pit to you today. Then express your commitment to believe that because He is at work, the outcome will be amazing.

From Misery to Ministry

Rejoice in the Lord always. I will say it again: Rejoice!

—Philippians 4:4

When Paul says we are to rejoice in everything, he isn't insisting that we *like* our circumstances. He doesn't demand that we pretend our circumstances aren't so bad, when in fact they are really lousy. But in the midst of longing for deliverance, and in the thick of praying for God to intervene, Paul still says, "Rejoice." He doesn't say, "I will put on mask and do a darn good performance of being oh-so-happy." Rather, he speaks of a joy that comes from being able to see beyond the current misery to the opportunity tucked within the moment.

I often fall far short of Paul's perspective, yet his example gives me a renewed purpose in each place I go and with each person God puts in my path. It forces me not to react in the way that would feel good but rather in a way that does good. It makes me rethink the difficult situations I face. Little by little, I realize it's OK that I'm not happy about the situations I'm in, but there is joy to be discovered as I allow God to use me while I'm there.

In what ways is God inviting you to see that your life is more than misery—it's your mission field?

The Three Cs

Oh, how I love your law! I meditate on it all day long.

—PSALM 119:97

Sometimes when we read our Bibles, it's useful to have an aid of some sort to help us absorb what we've read. One aid that helps me is the following: The Three Cs.

Comforting. What is comforting in this passage? What encourages me and helps me stand strong?

Challenging. What step forward is God asking me to take? Is there a new way of thinking that God wants me to adopt? Is there a command to obey? Is there a behavior or attitude God wants me to let go of? Is there a lie God wants me to replace with truth?

Contemporary. In what way is this passage relevant to my twenty-first-century life?

Not every C will apply to every passage you read. And the questions I've listed are just suggestions to get you started. Make this aid your own. Customize it (another C!) as you see fit. I share it with you simply in hopes that it will enrich the time you spend enjoying God's Word.

Read a portion of God's Word today, perhaps a psalm or a chapter from a Gospel or one of the New Testament letters, such as Philippians or 1 Peter. What verses were comforting, challenging, or contemporary in your everyday life?

Send Me!

"Here am I. Send me!"
—ISAIAH 6:8

What qualifies you for God's great work? Is it a childhood of perfect church attendance? Is it your knowledge of the Bible? Is it your great singing voice? Maybe it's your social standing or how many volunteer hours you've racked up.

No! Here's a great truth: The one qualifier for a believer to be chosen for God's daily work is availability. As we make ourselves available, God promises to work in and through our lives in greater ways than anything we can imagine.

Today you and I can echo the Old Testament prophet Isaiah: "Here we are, Lord. Send us. To the weary clerk at the supermarket, to the homeless woman at the shelter, to an orphan in Haiti, to the neighbor going through a divorce. Send us."

I'm available. How about you?

Here I am, Lord. Ready to serve you. Where would you have me go?

Butterfly Friends

Above all, keep fervent in your love for one another.
—1 PETER 4:8 NASB

On the morning after a family wedding, several of us were enjoying breakfast outdoors. My mother-in-law spotted a butterfly, which was hardly unusual. But what was unusual was her curiosity about that butterfly. "What kind is it?" she asked us. "Look at its markings! Could it be a monarch?"

I saw a generic butterfly. She saw a unique creature and wanted to know more about it. I was with a woman who notices life's everyday treasures.

How often do our friends become like butterflies? We grow so conditioned to having them around that we don't truly see them: their uniqueness, their beauty, the specific sort of treasures they bring to our lives.

Without your friends, who would listen to you, even when you're on a rant? Who would give you good advice? Who would share a pint of ice cream with you when you're blue? Who would you trust with your secrets? Who would pick you up when you're down? Who would laugh with you when you're silly? Who would come running the moment you say, "Help"?

Reflect on the treasures your friends bring to your life. How can you be a treasure to _____ (friend's name)? Make a separate list for each person.

Who Knows?

Jesus wept.

—JOHN 11:35

Who knows the challenges you face today? Who knows you are lonely? Who knows how terrified you are? Who knows your financial distress, the hidden addiction, the depression hiding behind the big smile and cute shoes? Who knows that you are barely holding on?

Jesus knows.

Jesus wept with Mary and Martha when their brother Lazarus died. He didn't cry because He didn't know how to handle the situation or was not in control of it. Jesus knew He would soon restore life to Lazarus. Yet He cared so deeply for Mary and Martha that He went to them, listened, and wept.

He will listen to you too. Run to Him today.

"Jesus wept" is not only the shortest verse in the Bible; it is also the title of a song performed by Sia. While the publicity-averse singer has not disclosed information about her faith, the song portrays Christ's humanity in a personal way that offers a unique perspective. Both the audio version and lyrics are available online.

Value Added

But whatever were gains to me I now consider loss
for the sake of Christ.

—PHILIPPIANS 3:7

Most of us are familiar with how dramatically Saul's behavior changed when he met Christ on the Damascus road. The persecutor of Christ's followers was also known as Paul, the great missionary and teacher and prolific letter writer.

But let's not miss another profound change in Paul's life—the change in his values. He describes that change in his letter to the Philippians. His values once focused on religious piety, family pedigree, education, and professional success. Worthy values, but they became rubbish to him after he met Christ.

His new value was simple. Only one thing mattered. To know Christ. And as a result of knowing Christ, to become more like Him.

Take some time today to explore how your values have changed since you met Jesus as Lord. What did you once value that doesn't matter to you any longer? What do you value now that held no interest for you in the past? Thank God that you, like Paul, are a "new creation" (2 Corinthians 5:17). That's a value-added proposition!

Twists and Turns

Trust in the LORD will all your heart and lean not on
your own understanding; in all your ways submit to him,
and he will make your paths straight.

—PROVERBS 3:5–6

"I've never met a person for whom there was a straight path
to success. Rather, there are ups and down, twists and
turns. You just have to keep on keeping on." My husband has
spoken these words to our boys many times through the years
when they've found life to be a twisted and tangled road to
navigate.

When your path starts to resemble Lombard Street in San
Francisco, let God take over. Your job is to trust; His job is to
"make your paths straight."

*What twist are you experiencing in your path today? What
would it look like to submit to God with your whole heart and
leave the twist in His hands?*

Be a Reaper

Let us not become weary in doing good, for at the proper
time we will reap a harvest if we do not give up.
—GALATIANS 6:9

Each time my family moves, I am reminded of how easy it
is to give up. You see, as I clean out closets and shelves, I
run across evidence of all the projects I deserted at the halfway point. Halfway is where excitement can wane, perhaps
because I can't quite see the end yet. So I lose motivation and
set projects aside *temporarily*, intending to return to them after a bit of a rest. Funny how easily I can forget those projects
entirely. Out of sight, out of mind?

If not for the great promise in today's passage, we could
grow discouraged by the projects we don't quite complete,
the goals we don't quite accomplish. Let Paul's reminder spur
us on. As we keep on keeping on, we *will* reap a harvest. We
just have to do what we know to do and wait patiently on
God's timing.

*If you haven't already done so, make a list of the projects
you'd like to accomplish by the end of this year. Keep it
simple. Then ask God for the necessary patience and endurance to see you through.*

What a Coincidence!

"And who knows but that you have come to your
royal position for such a time as this?"

—ESTHER 4:14

As I read through the book of Esther recently, I noticed that God's name is never mentioned. Esther's story is filled with drama, romance, intrigue, suspense … but no God.

I once read that coincidences are merely God's way of doing things anonymously. And Esther's story is filled with "coincidences." Was it mere coincidence that Queen Vashti would not follow the king's orders? Was King Xerxes' insomnia a coincidence? Was it a coincidence that Mordecai overheard the plot to kill the king? No, God was at work behind the scenes in the lives of Vashti, Mordecai, the king, and many others.

And today it's no coincidence that you live in your particular state, city, and neighborhood. It's no coincidence that you are part of a certain school system, church, community center, tennis group, book club. Like Esther, you were put there "for such a time as this." And God didn't just drop you there and leave. He is there with you. He is at work behind the scenes of your life.

Watch for "coincidences" that come your way today and step into them with the faith and courage of Esther.

The Worry Hour

"Can any one of you by worrying add
a single hour to your life?"
—MATTHEW 6:27

I have always been a worrier. I mean, worry is essential. Right? If I worry, it won't happen (like carrying an umbrella so it won't rain). If I *don't* worry, the world may spin off its axis.

I once confessed my worry to a professor, who responded by giving me an assignment. Every day I was to designate a worry time. During the rest of the day I would say no to worry. But when the "worry hour" arrived, I would do nothing but worry. No TV, no reading, no crosswords—just worrying.

At first it felt so freeing to have an hour to dedicate to my favorite pastime of worrying. After a few days, however, I noticed that my "worry hour" wasn't changing anything. It wasn't protecting my kids. It wasn't healing anyone of disease. It wasn't adding one moment to my life. In fact, it was actually taking valuable moments away from my life.

Soon, the "worry hour" grew shorter and shorter. So these days, if something is truly eating at me, I return to that ritual the professor taught me but only long enough to get perspective.

Read Matthew 6:25–34 in your Bible. Then tell a friend what you've discovered about worry.

Better Than Whistling

Come, let us bow down in worship,
let us kneel before the LORD our Maker.

—PSALM 95:6

Remember the song "Whistle While You Work" from *Snow White and the Seven Dwarfs*? It's fun and perky, but most of the time, whistling just isn't enough.

Some days at work (whether we're working at home or away from home) everything we do feels empty. Everything we say sounds sharp. We feel underappreciated, worn out, used up. We can't stop wondering why work isn't as fulfilling for us as it seems to be for everyone else. No amount of whistling is going to fix that degree of discouragement.

Isaiah 40 seems to understand how we feel, and it offers a solution far more powerful than whistling. Verse 9 begins a section that reminds us what kind of God we worship, then ends with the proclamation "Here is your God!" Each verse that follows paints a picture of incomparable power, greatness, and awesomeness, until Isaiah declares: "Those who hope in the Lord will renew their strength."

We don't overcome work-weariness and world-weariness by whistling. We overcome it by worshiping.

When work threatens to overwhelm me today, help me to worship you, the God who loves me and fills my work with purpose and power beyond what I can imagine.

What God Will Never Say

The words of the LORD are flawless, like silver purified
in a crucible, like gold refined seven times.

—PSALM 12:6

I write often about being still and listening to God. But if
your relationship with God is still fairly new, you may feel
nervous about how to discern His voice from your own or
from the subtle lies of the world around you.

You discern God's voice the way your physician goes
about diagnosing your condition—by ruling things out. We
can avoid a lot of confusion by taking into account what God
will *not* say to us:

God will never condemn us (Romans 8:1). If you're hearing things like "Shame on you" or "Look at the mess you've
made," it's not God speaking.

God will never tempt us (James 1:13). He may allow trials to come our way to make us stronger, but He will never
induce us to sin.

God will never contradict the teachings of the Bible. God
won't change His mind about what He has said to us through
His inspired Word.

*"God is not human, that he should lie, not a human being,
that he should change his mind. Does he speak and then not
act? Does he promise and not fulfill?" (Numbers 23:19).
How does that verse shape your view of what God is like?*

None Like You

Among the gods there is none like you, LORD;
no deeds can compare with yours.

—PSALM 86:8

Why do we worship God—the Supreme Being, the Master, the Creator? Pastor Joel Lindsey writes, "The goal of adoration is to offer our highest compliments to God. Prayers of adoration are prayers of praise for who God is, what He's done, what He's doing, and what He will accomplish in and for His people."

David models this type of prayer in Psalm 86: 8–10 (MSG): "There's no one quite like you among the gods, O Lord, and nothing to compare with your works. All the nations you made are on their way, ready to give honor to you, O Lord, ready to put your beauty on display, parading your greatness, and the great things you do—God, you're the one, there's no one but you!"

Here's something you can ponder today: In what false gods have you trusted in the past? How did they let you down? How has God proven superior to those false gods? Let these reflections inspire you with praise for a God like no other god—your God.

God Can Work with That

"With man this is impossible, but not with God;
all things are possible with God."

—MARK 10:27

Are your masks firmly in place? If so, I'm here to tell you
that God has called you to much more than a life of
hiding and self-protection. He wants to work in your life in
ways that may seem impossible to you but are a cinch for the
God of the universe. It is a lie to think you are too messed up
or it is too late to be a part of His plan for you. With God,
nothing—even the transformation of your burdens—is impossible.

All those repulsive, hurtful bits of you that shout condescending messages—they don't intimidate Jesus. All the
mistakes, sins, hurts, abuses, abandoned dreams—He wades
right on through, proclaiming, "I can work with that!" What
you or others may deem spiritually catastrophic, Jesus stands
ready and able to put to use.

I'll say it again: With God, nothing is impossible.

*What burdens are you carrying today? Write them down
during your quiet time with the Lord today. And know this:
regardless of your wounds, failures, and sins, you may be on
the verge of becoming God's greatest miracle. Will you believe
He can reverse your burdens to blessings?*

It's My Right!

"I have the right to do anything," you say—
but not everything is beneficial.

—I CORINTHIANS 10:23

When my boys were young, I often said to them, "Just because you can doesn't mean you should."

Similarly, we are legally free to do many things in our society, but that doesn't mean those things are befitting someone who calls Jesus her Lord.

Philippians 2:3–4 guides us in exercising our freedom: "Do nothing out of selfish ambition or vain conceit. Rather, in humility value others above yourselves, not looking to your own interests but … to the interests of the others." Then, Paul describes how Jesus modeled this, dying on the cross for us even though He had the right to refuse such humiliation.

Freedom is a gift best exercised not for our own sakes, but for the sake of others. And I believe freedom is best *enjoyed* when used to benefit others instead of ourselves. Try it and see.

What is one way you can exercise your freedom in Christ in a way that benefits someone else today?

Brain Blips

Though outwardly we are wasting away,
yet inwardly we are being renewed day by day.

—2 CORINTHIANS 4:16

An elderly husband and wife both keep forgetting things. The man gets up to go to the kitchen. The wife asks, "Where are you going?"

He says, "To the kitchen."

She asks, "Will you be so kind as to get me a small bowl of vanilla ice cream? With strawberries?" Then she adds, "Do you think you should write this down?"

He says, "No, I can remember that."

"But I'd also like some whipped topping," she says, "so maybe you'd better make a list."

"No, no, no," he says, "I've got it. Vanilla ice cream, strawberries, and whipped topping."

When he returns to the living room, he hands his wife a plate of bacon and eggs.

"Oh my goodness," she cries. "You forgot the toast!"

Moral: Every time we forget something, we're reminded that "outwardly we are wasting away." But thank the Lord that "inwardly we are being renewed day by day."

Celebrate your inward renewal today with some strawberries—or bacon. And don't forget the toast!

Theology Made Simple

This is love: not that we loved God, but that he loved us
and send his Son as an atoning sacrifice for our sins.

—1 JOHN 4:10

As I mentioned in the Valentine's Day devotional, the great theologian Karl Barth was asked near the end of his life, "Of all the theological insights you have ever had, which do you consider the greatest?" He replied, "The greatest theological insight that I have ever had is this: Jesus loves me, this I know, for the Bible tells me so."

This man who possessed knowledge that you and I can't even imagine found the message of a child's song to be more important and more wondrous than anything else he discovered in a lifetime of notable scholarship. The basic truths remain the basic truths whether we are two or ninety-two.

In Barth's response, we see an ingredient of childlike faith: simplicity. Children don't overcomplicate things. No "what ifs." No "if onlys." Jesus knew what we often forget: Simplicity isn't the same as shallowness. We often find the greatest depth in simplicity. A child may not be able to quote the Bible or find verses in the Bible, but a child is able to accept what matters most: Jesus loves me.

Can you sing "Jesus Loves Me"? If not, learn the song from a little child ... or someone with childlike faith.

Say Yes!

"Go; I will … teach you what to say."
—EXODUS 4:12

Let's pop in on the scene in Exodus 3–4. After calling Moses by name, God opened Moses's eyes to the needs of the hurting people around him. Then He invited Moses to be His chosen instrument to bring hope and healing to these suffering people.

What followed demonstrates that God has not robotically programed us to be at His service. He issues the invitation and then waits as we make our choice. We can see from the questions Moses asks that God even addresses our insecurities and excuses, things like: "But who am I, that I should go?" "But I have never been an eloquent speaker." "Can't someone else do it?" Does any of this sound like your inner dialogue when God invites you to serve?

I don't think God would have it any other way. I think He wants us to pause and work through our insecurities so that, at the end of the day, we understand this very important truth: Whatever God calls us to do, He has our back. I've always found that my lack of Kim-confidence makes way for a whole lot of God-confidence.

I know you're no Moses. Nobody is. But how is God calling you today to begin a conversation of hope with someone who is hurting?

Oh, Where Is My Hairbrush?

> If I must boast, I will boast of the things
> that show my weakness.
> —2 CORINTHIANS 11:30

A recent incident reminded me that I still have lots of room to grow. While dressing for an event in Florida, I was mentally rehearsing some messages I need to hear again and again. You know, *Free yourself to be yourself. Just be you, the true and authentic you.* I was on a roll!

But when I reached for my hairdryer, panic overcame me: I had left my round hairbrushes at home. "My hair!" I gasped. "What am I going to look like?" Then it hit me. I was going to look like … me.

There's nothing wrong with looking our best. But my moment of panic reminded me that I'm still working on this "free to be me" thing. I guess I could have beat myself up for being so shallow as to be a slave to a hairbrush. But instead I quoted Joyce Meyer: "I may not be where I want to be, but thank God I'm not where I used to be!"

By the way, I made it through the day without frightening anyone with my hairdo.

Look up "Free to Be Me" by Francesca Battistelli. Or, if you're feeling silly, sing along as Larry the Cucumber belts out "The Hairbrush Song" by Veggie Tales.

Pearls

I pray that you, being rooted and established in love,
may ... grasp how wide and long and high
and deep is the love of Christ.

—EPHESIANS 3:17–18

Once upon a time, there was a little girl who loved her strand of imitation pearls. Each evening her dad would read her a bedtime story, then look at his princess and ask, "Do you love me enough to give me those pearls?" She would nervously tuck them behind her back, holding on because she loved them ever so much.

The same routine continued for many months. One evening, her dad asked again, "Do you love me enough to give me your pearls?" After a long, thoughtful pause, and trying desperately to hold back tears, the little girl slowly brought her hand from behind her back and spilled forth the tarnished strand of pearls.

Her tears of sadness soon turned to tears of delight as she saw why her dad had been asking all along for her treasure. His intent was not to take it away from her, but rather to offer a greater treasure in exchange. For from His hands into hers slid a new strand of *real* pearls.

What imitation treasures hinder you from experiencing a greater treasure? Start each day asking your Father, "What is the pearl You want to give me today?"

Have an Abundant Day

The grace of our Lord was poured out on me abundantly,
along with the faith and love that are in Christ Jesus.

—1 TIMOTHY 1:14

As I write this, I'm sitting with my coffee looking over beautiful Lake Norman. That's about as good as it gets! Yet I'm reminded that my happiness does not lie in a lakeside vacation or any other material version of abundance, but rather in the abundance of God's promises.

God's arms overflow with His abundance for us every day. When He gives spiritual gifts to us, He gives in abundance. When He blesses us, He blesses in abundance. When we turn to Him with our hurts or confusion, His arms are opened wide with welcome, and His comfort is abundant. It is far, far deeper and wider than the lake before me.

You'd expect to pay a high price for such abundance, wouldn't you? The truth is, *none* of us can purchase God's abundance. It doesn't matter how much you have to offer—it is not for sale. Instead, against all human logic, the abundance of God is free—free to all who ask for it.

In what area of your life do you long to experience God's abundance today? Ask for it and then watch what happens.

Do Be Do Be Do

We are therefore Christ's ambassadors,
as though God were making his appeal through us.

—2 CORINTHIANS 5:20

You awaken to a high calling this morning: an ambassador! God has chosen you to be His personal representative. It's an awesome appointment and carries with it an awesome challenge. The apostle Paul describes it as the challenge "to live a life worthy of the calling."

What does that life look like? Some answers are found in Ephesians 4:2: "Be completely humble and gentle; be patient, bearing with one another in love."

Notice there are no "do" words here. The key word is "be." There's something about twenty-first-century life that spurs us to do, do, do. But what would happen if you were to "be" more than "do"?

Instead of focusing on what you need to do today, ask God to show you the kind of person He wants you to be today.

May

The Power of Determination

Ezra had determined to study and obey the Law
of the Lord and to teach those decrees
and regulations to the people of Israel.

—EZRA 7:10 NLT

We all have determination. Some of us are determined to get into last year's cute white capris in time for our beach vacation. Some of us are determined to master that new software program. Some of us are determined to run a marathon on our fiftieth birthday. Some of us are determined to ace our CPA exam.

Ezra had been chosen by God to be a leader and example for Israel during a time of turmoil. The task must have felt overwhelming, but Ezra seems to have focused on three "determinations":

- to study God's Word
- to obey God's Word
- to teach God's Words to the people around him

Did Ezra's determination make a difference? Read Ezra 10 to find out.

What are you determined to do with God's Word today? Read it? Do what it says? Tell someone else what you learned?

Simple Joys

The cheerful heart has a continual feast.

—PROVERBS 15:15

As Mother's Day approaches I always enjoy reminiscing about special moments with my two guys, Trey and Austin, who are now grown and living away from home.

I like to recall the look of accomplishment on their faces just after hitting a home run. I can still hear their giggles as they watched Dad do his funny dances. I still see their sheepish grins as they prepared for first dates.

A few years ago I asked them, "What is your favorite childhood memory?"

Without hesitation, they swapped big smiles. "Oh, Mom," Trey began, "Austin and I loved rainy days!"

I'm sure I looked confused because Austin said, "Don't you remember, Mom? As the rain began you would call us to the front door. We would drop whatever we were doing and race to get there. As you swung the door open, we would belly-flop onto the wet ground."

"Yes!" chimed in Trey, laughing.

Making memories with your child often merely requires recognizing a special moment and enjoying it together.

What are some of your favorite "rainy-day memories" from childhood or parenting?

Giving Notice

We are God's handiwork,
created in Christ Jesus to do good works,
which God prepared in advance for us to do.

—EPHESIANS 2:10

Have you done your "good works" today? I hear you groaning! But if you read on, I think you may gain a fresh perspective on good works. (Hint: You don't have to sell all you own and become a missionary in some far reach of the globe.)

Sometimes, the mightiest act of your day is simply to notice someone. That encounter may, after all, be a divine appointment prepared by God, specifically for you.

Look, really look, at the people God places in your path today. A discouraged coworker, a heartbroken teenager, a weary cashier. Will you look into his or her eyes and speak a word of encouragement or comfort before you move on to your next chore or coffee date?

No Matter What

> "Though he slay me, yet will I hope in him."
> —JOB 13:15

Just when we're about to lose hope, Job's life reminds us to expect God to do good things.

Job loved God and obeyed Him. Yet he lost everything. How easily he could have declared God's unfairness or demanded to know, "Why me?" But rather than choosing bitterness or giving up hope, Job chose to get up every morning and do what He knew God wanted him to do that day. His conduct sent the message, *No matter my circumstances, I have hope in God.* In the end, God not only turned around Job's calamity, but He also restored to Job twice what he had in the beginning (Job 42:12).

What seems unfair to you? Hopeless? Find hope today in Job's example and in God's promised restoration in your life.

Be Nice to My Friend

Encourage one another
and build each other up.
—I THESSALONIANS 5:11

Two women were chatting one day. One was being critical of herself, mulling over an area in her life where she felt she didn't measure up. The other woman interrupted and said, "Hey, you be nice to my friend! I like her; you should too."

What a great way to encourage those around us who verbally bully themselves day after day by only seeing the negative! How nice to have friend or be one who takes such a stand.

Listen to those around you. How can you encourage your friends and loved ones when they sound like verbal bullies? Proverbs 25:11 (NKJV) says, "A word fitly spoken is like apples of gold in settings of silver." Hand out some golden apples today.

Glorious Giggles

A cheerful heart is good medicine.

—PROVERBS 17:22

A friend of mine wages a great battle. Indescribable hurt and devastation have been unjustly heaped upon her family. Only God, her family, and her best friend know her deep turmoil and agony. Only they could speak adequately of the sleepless nights and spent tears. Yet she insists on protecting her family by finding reasons to laugh together.

Research shows that laughing will reduce your stress, increase your tolerance for pain, release infection-fighting antibodies, boost your attentiveness, and accelerate your energy. Good medicine, indeed.

Beyond all that, finding a reason to giggle today can glorify God. It proclaims to those who hear you that you believe He is about to accomplish more than you have asked, or even thought to ask, through His mighty power at work in you and in each circumstance that touches your life. So get your giggle on.

Before you go to bed tonight, describe in your journal something that made your heart cheerful today. In fact, you might want to make a Laugh List a nightly habit. Wouldn't it be fun to hit the pillow with your head filled with memories of the day's laughter!

The Time Is Right

There is a proper time ... for every matter,
though a person may be weighed down by misery.
—ECCLESIASTES 8:6

If the misery of your past is weighing you down, and you realize at last that you're not OK, you're right where you need to be.

If your present circumstances have stopped you in your tracks, leaving you paralyzed with fear and frustration, disappointment and disillusionment, you're right where you need to be.

If you're contemplating a future that holds more challenges than your faint heart can bear, never mind. You're right where you need to be.

If you're ready to offer God all of your life and ask Him to transform your burdens into blessings in ways you cannot begin to imagine, then you're right where God wants you to be!

Don't waste time today on regrets that you didn't deal sooner with the burdens in your life. Instead, shoot up hourly prayers of thanksgiving to God for bringing you to this place and time: right where He wants you to be.

A Pinch of Variety

You, God, are my God, earnestly I seek you.
—PSALM 63:1

You and your friends don't do exactly the same thing at exactly the same place every time you meet, do you? You may have book group friends that you also meet sometimes for lunch. You may have tennis friends with whom you also like to shop. Yet when we meet with God, we get the idea that we must follow a rigid structure that never varies. Not so!

When I was a young mom, my "quiet time" with God sometimes consisted of sticking printed verse cards on the diaper table and refrigerator where I could see them numerous times a day. I'd pray as I rocked one of the boys or while I showered. Once the boys entered school and car pools became a regular feature of my life, I'd keep an extra Bible in my car with some writing paper. Then I could read, write, and pray while waiting in line. Now I like to run with God in the morning. It's a twist on the old hymn "He Walks with Me." Well, God runs with me!

How will you spend time with God today? Where? What will you talk about? Try something or some place new to keep your relationship fresh. After all, it's the most important relationship you have.

Pushing Buttons

You turned my wailing into dancing;
you removed my sackcloth and clothed me with joy.
—PSALM 30:11

I need routine. Normally I get up early and write, then slip into running shoes for my special time with God. That "God and me" time is where, so often, I get hints about the next day's writing topic.

But being out of town can really mess with that routine. One morning, as I made my way down the hotel corridor to the elevator, my head was full of chatter. *I cannot believe I didn't run today. What am I supposed to write? This is a mess. Wait a minute! How long have I been in this elevator?* Yep, there I was on a glorious North Carolina morning, stuck in an elevator. Stuck! Then I realized I hadn't pushed the button.

Being stuck in that elevator is a lot like worry-induced paralysis. We fret about what we have done or haven't done or are going to do—and rely too little on what God can do. Just as I finally pushed the elevator's button to continue my journey, so you can push the button of His truth and experience the joy of moving forward.

Today, give yourself a break. Quit worrying. You're not perfect. You're going to fail. But your failures can't stop God's will in your life.

Help Is on the Way

"We do not know what to do,
but our eyes are upon you."

—2 CHRONICLES 20:12

I love the story of Jehoshaphat from the Old Testament. A day came when Jehoshaphat and his people found themselves under attack from a strong army. With no way to protect his people, Jehoshaphat called upon the Lord with the above prayer.

So many times I think about Jehoshaphat when I feel overwhelmed and powerless. When I have no idea what to do, I try to follow his lead by focusing on God and waiting on Him with confidence that His help is on the way.

Waiting is not easy when a battle is raging around you. But take your cue from Jehoshaphat: Whatever the battle, after you have done all you can do, focus on God and allow Him to fight for you.

What battle do you face today? What seems overwhelming? A difficult relationship? Financial hardships? The loss of a loved one? Scheming coworkers? Whatever the challenge may be, submit your requests to God in prayer.

Soul Cleansing

"My prayer is not that you take them out of the world
but that you protect them from the evil one.
They are not of this world, even as I am not of it.
Sanctify them by the truth; your word is truth."

—JOHN 17:15–17

Physical detox is designed to release toxins from the body to make you feel healthier, stronger, and more vibrant. But another type of toxin exists that is hazardous to our *souls*.

Every day, we walk through toxic attitudes, behaviors, and cultural influences that perhaps we are not even aware have attached to us. God already understands that we are going to get dirty as we run around in the world, just like we got dirty as children when our mothers let us play outdoors. Like the loving parent He is, He has made a way to protect us and keep our souls healthy and thriving. "Sanctify them by the truth," Jesus prayed. He knew firsthand what it was like to live in a contaminating world, and the words of His Father are the best spiritual cleanser one could find.

Have you grown tired of spiritual practices that used to fill your soul but now seem empty? Are you negative about life, sluggish, or apathetic? Are you compromising "just a little"? If so, let the Father sanctify you by His truth.

Name That Toxin

> "Though your sins are like scarlet,
> they shall be as white as snow; though they are
> red as crimson, they shall be like wool."
> —ISAIAH 1:18

It's impossible to stay clean for long. We wash our faces, we go to the gym, we need to wash our faces again. We wash our hands, we weed the garden, we wash our hands again.

Spiritual cleanliness is similar. All kinds of toxic influences swirl around us, and we can't always avoid being soiled by some of them. How do we stay clean?

First, it helps to name the toxin. Is it a critical spirit? Irritability? Apathy? Gossip? Anger? Next, identify the source of that toxin. Sometimes we can avoid toxins by avoiding certain places or TV shows or people. Or by not discussing politics! Last, release the toxin to God. Ask Him to cleanse you. "Create in me a pure heart, O God, and renew a steadfast spirit within me" (Psalm 51:10). You can't clean yourself, but God can cleanse you "by the washing with water through the word" (Ephesians 5:26).

What contamination have you picked up? Name it. Where did it come from? In what tangible way can you release it to God?

Life Is Good

The one who gets wisdom loves life;
the one who cherishes understanding
will soon prosper.
—PROVERBS 19:8

Do you love life? Are you filled with contentment? Can you step back at the end of a day, look at what you accomplished and did not accomplish, and still say, "Life is good"? If you are that kind of person, then you have been blessed with one of the gifts of wisdom. Godly contentment is a gift from God that allows us to be OK with where we are.

I'm not talking about self-satisfaction. We always want to keep growing. But we're content with where we are today. We're OK with ourselves because we know we're OK with God. Inhale that thought. Now, exhale contentment. And repeat.

"Blessed are those who find wisdom, those who gain understanding" (Proverbs 3:13). So count your blessings today. Literally. How many did you come up with?

Feeling Special

You are a chosen people, a royal priesthood,
a holy nation, God's special possession.

—1 PETER 2:9

Recently I was in Texas for a speaking tour. As my friend Karen drove us through town, I noticed people were pointing at us. I said to her, "I know we took some extra time getting dressed this morning, but, girl, I had no idea we were looking this good." About that time I looked up and saw a one-way sign. We were going the wrong way.

Life has a way of putting us in our place, doesn't it? Yet I'm encouraged by this incident. There was a time when my first thoughts would have been fearful: *What am I doing wrong? Why are people looking at me? Where can I hide?*

But my gracious God has, through the years, filled me with such a strong sense of His love that I could actually imagine—for a moment—that I was indeed special enough to earn stares from strangers. I didn't fear the stares; I enjoyed them. And of course, I had a good laugh at myself.

Loving God, take me from cringing to confident. Give me a confidence that is not shaken by how the world looks at me, because it is rooted in how you look at me: with perfect love, acceptance, and pleasure.

Sustaining Words

The Sovereign LORD has given me
a well-instructed tongue, to know
the word that sustains the weary.

—ISAIAH 50:4

When my boys were young and going off to school each day, I was careful to send them off with the right words. I wanted them to hear from me something that would be a happy reminder of who they were and what kind of home they'd be returning to at the end of the school day. I wanted to give them words that would sustain them out there in the big old world. I wanted my parting words to be like a hug.

When we start our day with reading God's Word, something similar happens. We have that "hug" of His love and truth and wisdom to get us through the stressful day ahead. Plus, we have His sustaining words to pass along to others who need a hug. The blessings multiply! Doesn't that make you want to open your Bible right now?

The second part of Isaiah 50:4 says, "He wakes me up in the morning, wakes me up, opens my ears to listen" (MSG). What's the first thing you think about when you wake up? When you start your day tomorrow, listen to what God wants to say through His Word.

Here and Now

"Here is my servant, whom I uphold,
my chosen one in whom I delight."

—ISAIAH 42:1

Do you ever have mornings when your waking thought is, *Who am I and why am I here?* God has an answer for you. You are …

- called by Him
- chosen by Him
- upheld by Him
- delighted in by Him

You are right where you need to be to have immediate access to His enduring strength, wisdom, and rest. How does that change your perspective on the day ahead?

In "He Knows My Name," Francesca Battistelli sings about her identity as a forgiven, chosen, and wanted child of the King. Look up the song's lyrics to find out more about how the singer knows she's adored by her heavenly Father.

Slaves to Yes

"All you need to say is simply 'Yes' or 'No.'"
—MATTHEW 5:37

I always smile when I remember a lunch date with a dear friend a few years ago. I was having a horrid migraine and had left home with no medicine. Because her husband was a dentist, she always carried in her purse samples of over-the-counter pain relievers. She dumped all she had on our small restaurant table. We were looking intently at our options when a man walked by and gasped. "Oh, just say no, ladies, just say no."

Let's face it: Women can be slaves to saying yes. We love to help, to please, to fix things. We hate to be perceived as selfish, unsociable, or self-indulgent. But it's OK to say no to many things in life, as that man reminded my friend and me.

You can be free from the pressure to say yes today. You can be free from explanations or invented excuses for saying no. How? By making it your habit to ask God first before you say yes—or no. He may want someone else to step up and serve. And He may be calling you to say no because there's something He wants you to say yes to tomorrow.

How many things are you doing today that you wish you had said no to when asked?

The Importance of First Steps

The end of a matter is better than its beginning.

—ECCLESIASTES 7:8

"Did you know you were broken?"

This question came up at one of my speaking engagements, and I thought carefully before answering.

"Yes, I knew my hurts and regrets, my unfilled hopes and dreams, but I thought I could fix myself. I thought if I worked hard enough and long enough I could present myself to the world as 'all better.' I had to learn that my first step toward real and lasting healing was presenting my broken self to those I trusted."

That step was one of the hardest of my life! It was work—no magic wands and fairy dust. But it was the first step to the real me and had I not taken it, I would have missed the best years of my life.

Don't settle for anything less than God's best for your life. Take heart in the truth of today's verse. We cannot change what brought us to this point of pain, but God promises we can determine a new ending. Yes, it takes a lot of courage, but you are stronger than you know, and God has such big plans for you!

Are you silently hurting? If so, I urge you to find someone you can trust and begin talking.

When the Earth Moves

No one can lay any foundation other than
the one already laid, which is Jesus Christ.

—1 CORINTHIANS 3:11

You may have experienced an actual earthquake. Or a ground-shifting feeling when your spouse asked for a divorce, or the doctor delivered his diagnosis, or a pink slip appeared on your desk. I suspect we all felt the ground shift on 9/11 or the first time we heard about ISIS.

Our gut-level response when the ground shifts is almost always emotional: shock, sadness, fear, anger. That's OK; God created us to have emotions. But we have choices to make. Will we play the blame game? ("This would never have happened if we still had prayer in school!") Will we withdraw and give in to paralysis? Will we become news junkies, glued to the TV (or Facebook) so we don't miss any "breaking news"?

I've been known to choose all those behaviors at once! But only one choice has ever proven effective when the ground shifts beneath my feet. I turn to the foundation that never shifts or shatters: Jesus Christ. Once I take my stand on His unshakeable foundation, I find the stability to step forward and press on. I am confident you will too.

The next time you get that feeling of the ground shifting
beneath you, turn your worry into prayer.

None Too Small

"Who dares despise the day of small things?"
—ZECHARIAH 4:10

'm going to confront a lie today. A subtle lie that will rob you of the very life you seek—the life filled with daily invitations to allow God's power to work through you to do infinitely more than you can think or imagine.

This lie says that what you're being asked to do is too small and insignificant, that it doesn't really matter, that you need not bother because it will make no difference anyway.

Remember when the disciples helped Jesus feed five thousand people with next to nothing? What if the disciples that day had believed the "it's too small" lie? What if they had ignored the shy lad with the meager lunch? Or what if, when challenged to give up his meal, the lad had believed his offering was too small, and declined? Truly, who could have imagined the difference his bread and fish were about to make?

Jesus could. Only He knows the difference His power can make through your life. It's time to untangle your mind from the size of the task to the real issue: your obedience to the task. God used the lad's meager offering to feed a multitude.

What have you deemed underwhelming that God has an overwhelming purpose for?

The Power to Care

He had compassion on them.

—MATTHEW 14:14

You are probably familiar with the miracle of Jesus feeding the five thousand, but did you know He worked that day from a broken heart? You see, shortly before the crowd's arrival, Jesus had been told of the violent beheading of His cousin John the Baptist. Jesus had come to an isolated location seeking a place of solitude where He could grieve. Yet, as He saw the crowds approaching, Jesus had compassion upon them. He set aside His grief, and He served them.

So many women I know show similar compassion amid pain. Some keep singing with a broken heart. Some keep laughing through fearful times. Some keep doing good for others even when their own illnesses demand so much of them.

To those who demonstrate such compassion, God has great things coming. Twelve baskets of food were left over after the multitude was fed. *Left over!* This abundance is what God has in store for those who see others in distress and care for their needs, even with a broken heart.

So keep your head up, and keep looking for those who need God's compassion. Pay attention to how God uses you today in spite of the burdens you carry (or more likely, because of them).

More than Money Can Buy

"Therefore, if you are offering your gift
at the altar and there remember that your brother
or sister has something against you, leave your gift
there in front of the altar. First go and be reconciled
to them; then come and offer your gift."

—MATTHEW 5:23–24

There's no way around the fact that God cares about how we get along with others. He views our relationships as being of much greater importance than the amount of the check we are about to write to our church. Imagine that!

And what's more, God is not concerned with who is at fault. He simply says go. Leave your money, leave your gifts, leave all the things that impress other people—and do what impresses God. Be reconciled.

Reconciliation is costly. It may cost us our pride. It may cost us the good opinion of others. It may cost us time and energy, especially emotional energy. But God paved the way when He paid the greatest possible price to make sure we were reconciled with Him. Maybe reconciliation with one another isn't so costly after all.

Who has something against you? What do you need to do today to be reconciled with that person?

Alone

Jesus often withdrew to lonely places and prayed.
—LUKE 5:16

*A*lone. That word can arouse a variety of emotions in us. For some, "alone" may mean loneliness or desolation. For others, it may speak of peace and quiet.

Interestingly, some of the most significant encounters with God in the Bible came during a time of aloneness.

Moses was alone, except for his father-in-law's sheep (Exodus 3:1–5).

John the Baptist was alone in the wilderness (Luke 1:80).

Cornelius was praying by himself when the angel came to him (Acts 10:1–3).

The disciple John was alone in Patmos when he received the revelations.

In each case, when God interrupted the solitude, He brought a gift: the gift of purpose. After each encounter, these men moved forward with a clearer grasp of how God wanted to work in and through them.

Let me encourage you today not to fear being alone, but to recognize it as an opportunity to be in conversation with God. You too may come away with a stronger sense of purpose for your life.

Where can you go to be alone with God?

Wisdom Personified

The LORD gives wisdom; from his mouth
come knowledge and understanding.

—PROVERBS 2:6

When we cry out for wisdom, we are crying out to a person, for God is the source of all wisdom. The pursuit of wisdom is the pursuit of a relationship—not a collection of information, not even knowledge. A relationship. With God.

The pursuit of knowledge has plenty of merit. We get smarter, we make better-informed decisions, we gain skills, we get perspective (think about how much your understanding of current events is impacted by how much knowledge you have or do not have about history). But as valuable as knowledge is, it is still just a thing. Wisdom is a *Person*.

Letting God run our lives—refusing to walk into a new day without Him—is perhaps the epitome of wisdom. What would that look like for you today?

The Right Fit

Your eyes saw my unformed body;
all the days ordained for me were written in your book.

—PSALM 139:16

One day when my cleaning lady and I were halfway through our weekly cleaning, I needed to run a quick errand. So I slipped some shoes on and dashed out the door.

Well, I got to the store, and after just a few steps I noticed that my feet hurt like crazy. *What is wrong with these shoes?* I wondered. I pressed on with my shopping, but by the time I left the store I was limping. My toes felt crunched, and I was miserable.

When I got back home, I said to my cleaning lady, "I don't know what's wrong with these shoes of mine. I had to take them off because they hurt so bad."

She burst out laughing. "You've got my shoes on!"

She wears a size 5. I wear a size 8. Ouch.

That's what it's like when we try to walk through life in someone else's shoes. We're never going to feel complete. We're never going to feel whole. We're never going to feel *comfortable!*

God says, "I gave you your shoes for a reason. Put them back on. I have a path laid out for you, and it's going to be a perfect fit." Thank Him for your uniqueness today.

Waiting Rooms

Wait for the LORD; be strong and take heart
and wait for the LORD.

—PSALM 27:14

Some of the best time I spend with God happens while I'm housecleaning. That may be the one time my brain goes on autopilot. I quit trying to organize my thoughts, and instead I let God direct my thinking and show me who I can pray for.

This morning I was thinking of all who are in the "waiting rooms" of life. Waiting for a phone call, waiting for a diagnosis, waiting for a college admission, waiting for a job, waiting for the right mate.

I'm in one of life's waiting rooms myself, and as I vacuumed the floor today, I contemplated possible outcomes and prepared myself for different scenarios. What about this, and what about that? Then I heard that familiar, gentle whisper: "But, Kim, what about me?" I smiled as my thoughts returned to our great God who sees it all, planned it all, and controls it all. As we all wait, friends, let's be of good courage, for our God is faithful to His word!

Help me, Lord, to "be strong and take heart and wait" for you. I put my trust in you, the one who is working all things to my good and your glory.

The Laughing Woman

She can laugh at the days to come.

—PROVERBS 31:25

I marvel at this verse. I've spent lots of time wondering what made this woman capable of laughing at the future. Didn't she know how unpredictable life is? How scary it is at times?

I believe this woman had been prescribed very special bifocals. I believe she could see God at work close up and also far away. In the present and in the future.

I believe her laugh was a laugh of peace. She was utterly certain that God would give her what she needed when she needed it. And I believe that you and I can have that same attitude as we spend time with God and grow familiar with His ways and His character.

Read the following verses about the Proverbs 31 woman: "Bold power and glorious majesty are wrapped around her as she laughs with joy over the latter days. Her teachings are filled with wisdom and kindness, as loving instruction pours from her lips. She watches over the ways of her household and meets every need they have" (vv. 25–27 TPT). Which attributes resonate with you?

Why Be a Wallflower?

If our hearts condemn us, we know that God
is greater than our hearts, and he knows everything.
—1 JOHN 3:20

Is anything lovelier than a bride dancing with her proud father? Did you know your heavenly Father is inviting you, His cherished daughter, to dance? Have you accepted His invitation today? If not, why not?

Often when God invites us to dance, our first impulse is look in the mirror to make sure everything is OK. But we don't see OK. We see every failure, careless word, foolish choice, act of rebellion, and every wound inflicted by us or against us. Magnified. And we conclude: *I'm not worthy to dance.*

Today's truth from 1 John says otherwise. God has set you free from all that: your latest mistake, dress size, marital problems. Anything that has driven you to hide from the dance.

God knows everything about you and still says, "Dance with me." Will you accept?

Look up the words to "Dance with Me" by Jesus Culture.
Which phrase or sentence from those lyrics connected most
with you?

Your Power Plan

"Now, who is willing to consecrate
themselves to the LORD today?"

—1 CHRONICLES 29:5

Many of us respond to our daily struggles with the emotion of the moment. We may compare ourselves to others, doubt our worth, or dwell on a harsh remark. But we aren't slaves to our emotions. The following power plan frees us to enjoy moment-by-moment abundant living:

Pray. Quiet your inner struggle with prayer. God promises to answer. Our part is to listen to His guidance and wisdom.

Lay out God's truth. Don't get caught up in assigning blame. Edit out every message except the one *God* gives you about the truth of your situation.

Analyze your options. Will you appear weak or odd in the world's eyes? Is a significant change of direction or attitude required? Are you willing to surrender to God's power even if it costs you?

Do what is *necessary*. You may still have unanswered questions. You may fear what others might think. But if you are surrendered to God's power, you will do whatever He calls you to do. And it will be worth it.

Surrender is not easy, so you need a plan—one that trains you, long before a crisis occurs, not to react, but to respond. What's yours? Write it down today.

In the Depths

If I go up to the heavens, you are there;
if I make my bed in the depths, you are there.

—PSALM 139:8

I hid my inner turmoil behind a mask for a long, long time.
But as I found the courage to be honest with God about
the burdens my heart carried, I found an amazing thing: God
wasn't put off by my hurts and pain. He was right in the midst
of them; He was waiting for me there!

Lord, you know everything there is to know about me.

You've examined my innermost being with your loving gaze.

You perceive every movement of my heart and soul,

and understand my every thought before it even enters
my mind.

You are so intimately aware of me, Lord.

You read my heart like an open book

and you know all the words I'm about to speak! (Psalm
139:1–4 TPT)

When we carry heavy burdens, we spend a lot of time "in
the depths." And too often, we assume God is absent from
the depths. But the Bible tells us otherwise.

*Set aside some time today to read Psalm 139:1–18. Then tell
God how thankful you are that He is with you—in the good
times and the bad.*

Need a Miracle?

You are the God who performs miracles;
you display your power among the peoples.
—PSALM 77:14

I had followed my usual routine. Rolled out of bed. Grabbed my coffee. Headed to the computer. Prayed. Wrote. I was ready to hit "send" when the computer shut down. All my work was lost! I needed a miracle!

We all know what to do in situations like this: Pray! And so I did: "Dear Jesus, please, please save this! Please!" (Computer still down.) "Dear Lord, I know you have called me to write; I know this is your will. Please help me!" (Computer dead.) "Dear Jesus, please restore this now!" Silence. "Lord, you know I've done all you have asked of me. I got up early. I tried my best. I … I … I … What in the world should I do now?" Then a message appeared on my screen: *Mail Waiting to Be Sent.* Huh?

I can't explain what happened, but I can tell you this: God hasn't shut down on you. He may seem silent, but He is there. All your hard work, all your obedience, all the hours you have prayed, and even your secret tears have not gone unnoticed by Him.

God is still in the miracle business. Your miracle, like my e-mail, is waiting to be sent. What do you need today?

June

The Real Lion

Be alert and of sober mind. Your enemy the devil prowls
around like a roaring lion looking for someone to devour.
—1 PETER 5:8

A lion's roar is intended to intimidate, to make its victim
feel threatened, helpless, hopeless. But no matter how
much your enemy roars, he cannot win. Why? First, you are
not a victim. According to 1 John 4:4, you're an overcomer,
because Christ, who is in you, is greater than the enemy who
is in the world. Second, Satan may be *like* a lion, but Jesus is
the Lion of Judah.

Consider the following quote from *The Lion, the Witch,
and the Wardrobe* describing Aslan, who symbolizes Jesus in
C. S. Lewis' The Chronicles of Narnia series:

Wrong will be right, when Aslan comes in sight,

At the sound of his roar, sorrows will be no more,

When he bares his teeth, winter meets its death,

And when he shakes his mane, we shall have spring again.

Satan is a counterfeit; he has no real power over you—
never has, never will. The roar—that's all he's got. When
your enemy comes looking for you today, he'll have to make
it past Jesus. And he won't.

*Compare Lewis's account of Aslan with Peter's description
of the devil. Then praise God that you serve a Master who is
gentle, loving, and mighty.*

What's Your Story?

Leaving her water jar, the woman went back to the town and said to the people, "Come, see a man who told me everything I ever did. Could this be the Messiah?"

—JOHN 4:28–29

In John chapter 4, Jesus meets a woman after he stops to rest at a well in the noonday sun. After asking her for a drink, he says, "Everyone who drinks this water will get thirsty again and again. Anyone who drinks the water I give will never thirst—not ever. The water I give will be an artesian spring within, gushing fountains of endless life" (vv. 13–14 MSG).

Jesus believed in the Samaritan woman. He had come to reveal His plan for her life. And because she *believed in Him* and welcomed His plan, Jesus accomplished an amazing transformation in a woman others had written off as insignificant and unworthy. But the story doesn't end there. The woman returned to town and started talking about what had happened to her. And because of her story, people believed. They embraced a Savior.

Take some time today to read the full story of the Samaritan woman in John 4:1–42. What's your story? How would you complete the sentence, "Come, see a man who _____"?

Slowpokes

Follow God's example … as dearly loved children.
—EPHESIANS 5:1

Some days I feel like a turtle. Any progress I may make seems slow, imperceptible. You see, I'm hard on myself, and you are probably hard on yourself. We are prisoners of our own expectations.

Today, remind yourself that you are God's child, and children have the freedom to go slow. When you began to follow your father around the house—crawling, perhaps, or wobbling on your toddler legs—did he berate you for being slower than he was? Did he fuss at you when you stumbled or fell on your diapered bottom? More likely, he laughed with pleasure that you wanted to follow him around. He cheered you on, didn't he?

Well, you have the greatest of all cheerleaders on your side. Your heavenly Father believes in you and delights in you. He knows that if you just keep taking those tiny steps toward Him, "as dearly loved children," you will get better and better at following His example. Your pace will quicken. Your steps will, in time, gain confidence. You'll lose your footing less often.

Even for slowpokes, progress happens!

Father God, thank you for being so patient with my turtle-like progress. When I long to be a hare who finishes fast, give me endurance to run the race in step with you.

Say No to Negativity

We demolish arguments and every pretension that sets
itself up against the knowledge of God, and we take
captive every thought to make it obedient to Christ.

—2 CORINTHIANS 10:5

How easily we slip into assuming the worst in life! We hit a rough patch in our marriages, and before long we're picturing ourselves divorced. Or we walk into a room, see a dismissive glance, and convince ourselves that everyone in the room is talking about us. For years, as I dealt with anorexia, I was certain that the smell of food would make my life reel out of caloric control, making me too obese to leave my home.

The Bible urges us to take our negative thoughts captive and turn them toward what is true. You're free to choose what you think about, you know. So choose truth.

Rather than assuming the worst, let's do an "I dare you" this week. I dare you to reject a negative thought when it enters your mind and to speak (yes, aloud) something positive.

Check In and Check Up

Teach us to number our days,
that we may gain a heart of wisdom.

—PSALM 90:12

We're almost halfway through this year. Can you believe it? It's so easy to start out the year with great resolve, and then, when we aren't even looking, it all flies past us. And we're left saying, "Huh? Really?"

Well, let's forget what's behind us. What's done is done. Let's look ahead, because there's still time to make the MOST of this year. Ready?

M. Ask God, each day, to help you focus your *mind* on His Word.

O. As you focus, look for the *opportunity* to do what His Word says (James 1:22).

S. Once you see your opportunity, don't run away. Instead, *step* into it.

T. Because, after all, you know you can *trust* God with the outcome.

Mind. Opportunity. Step. Trust. Those are your key words for making the MOST of the rest of this year.

Now's a good time in the year to perform a spiritual growth checkup. Where have you enjoyed the most progress? In which area would you most like to grow?

Be Available

> He who began a good work in you will carry it on
> to completion until the day of Christ Jesus.
>
> —PHILIPPIANS 1:6

When God called me to write, it was a much bigger task than what I knew I could do. So I asked God what He expected of me. He said, "Be available."

To make myself available I first placed my confidence in the promise of His power working through me. Next, I identified disciplines that could help me stay receptive to His power. This required commitment to small habits: rolling out of bed by 4:30 every morning—at home or away; eating healthy to insure energy; running each morning; declining invitations that would keep me up too late. As I was faithful in doing what little I could do, God was faithful in completing what He had promised to do.

You have that same promise of God's faithfulness today. If you're ready to act, He's ready too!

As you face the impossibility of whatever God may be asking of you—restoring a friendship, saving your marriage, beginning a Bible study at school, starting an exercise program, daring to reveal your secret hurt—identify what you can do. What changes in your mind-set, schedule, or lifestyle can you make to become more ready and available?

What If . . .

Put your hope in the LORD, for with the LORD
is unfailing love and with him is full redemption.

—PSALM 130:7

For a long time, when God presented me with an opportunity, my usual response was one of regret: "if only." Those "if onlys" were the lies I believed or the excuses I made for why I couldn't step out in faith and move on. "If only they'd let me stay with my granddad" was my biggest regret. You may have regrets like "If only I hadn't married this difficult man" or "If only I'd stayed in school."

"If onlys" are comfortable because they give us a reason to stay where we are: stuck. I stayed stuck for more than twenty years. But then Jesus asked me one day, "Kim, *what if* you just trusted Me? *What if* you took one little step? *What if* you dropped some of your pride and admitted to a friend that you're confused and hurting. *What if*, Kim?"

Jesus replaced my "if onlys" with a bunch of "what ifs"—invitations to see myself and my burdens as He does. He doesn't want to negate our burdens. He doesn't label any part of us as unusable or unacceptable. Instead, He says, "Tell me what hurts your heart, because I want to reverse that."

Tell God about your "if onlys" today.

Green Means Go, Part 1

"Here am I. Send me!"
—ISAIAH 6:8

"Green means *go*," my little grandniece told me one day at the pool. How right she is! Sometimes you just have to step out and *go* when God shows you what He wants you to do.

I remember when I decided to invite that first group of gals over for what they thought was just another coffee at Kim's house. As the day approached, I was having night sweats and stomach convulsions because I was worrying so much about exactly what it was God wanted me to do. And what did He want me to do? Step out and change the world? No. He had simply asked me to invite some women to my home and tell them what He was doing in my life.

Almost twenty-five years later I cannot thank God enough for giving me the guts to do what He asked. Back then, I was so green at doing God's will that I didn't have a clue what that meant. But I did know one thing: I was determined to find out.

Someone said, "Change only occurs when the pain of staying the same exceeds the pain of changing." Is there something inside calling you to more? When God calls you to a task, no matter how ill-prepared you may feel, green still means go!

Green Means Go, Part 2

He guides me along the right paths
for his name's sake.

—PSALM 23:3

Recall grandniece's repetitive declaration: "Aunt Gim, green means go!" Here's the rest of this story.

While this chant was swirling in my head, a woman sensed God inviting her to begin a COFFEE in her area.* "Really, God?" she asked. "I have never attended a COFFEE. So how can I possibly *start* one?" She needed confirmation that this was what He wanted her to do.

That day, she later told me, the traffic lights along her route home were all green. To her recollection, this had never happened before.

That same day, a friend of hers read my e-mail devotional titled "Green Means Go!" and felt prompted to forward it to her friend.

God wants to communicate with us.

Consider Psalm 23:1 (TPT): "The Lord is my Best Friend and my Shepherd. I always have more than enough." Then write your own prayer.

---

* Conversations of Friends of Faith to Encourage and Equip. For more information about a COFFEE near you (or how to start your own COFFEE), visit rosesandrainbows.org.

Two Boats and a Helicopter

He brought me out into a spacious place;
he rescued me because he delighted in me.

—PSALM 18:19

The floodwaters were rising fast. Everyone was rushing to get out of town. One old lady climbed up on her roof.

A farmer came by in a rowboat and asked her to get in. "No thanks," said the old lady. "God will save me."

Next a man in a speedboat saw her. "Come on in," he said. "No thanks," said the old lady. "God will save me."

Pretty soon she was standing on her brick chimney with water lapping at her feet. She looked up and saw a helicopter with a rope ladder. A woman leaned out. "Grab on!" she called. "No thanks!" yelled the old lady. "God will save me."

Well, the old woman drowned, and when she got to heaven, she asked God why He didn't save her. God looked her in the eye. "I sent you two boats and a helicopter."

If we get in deep water today, let's make sure we don't overlook the two boats and the helicopter that God sends to our rescue!

Lord, you loved the world so much that you sent Jesus to rescue it. Thank you for giving us—giving me—the precious gift of your only Son.

Hearing Aids

"My sheep hear my voice;
I know them, and they follow me."
—JOHN 10:27

Prior to Caller ID technology telling you who was calling you on the phone, how did you recognize your callers? If it was someone you knew well, had spent a lot of time with, or had talked to many times before, then you recognized her voice before she even told you her name, right? You didn't need to see her face. You didn't need the help of technology. You knew, because you had a relationship with her.

Similarly, we learn to recognize God's voice as our relationship with Him grows. You may not be able to see His face, you may not have heavenly Caller ID, but if you've spent time in His presence, talking with Him and listening to Him through what He says in His Word, you will soon discover that His voice is a familiar one. You know it's God speaking because, well, it just sounds like the God you've come to know.

Lord, teach me to hear your voice and recognize it, and to speak with you as a friend, just like Moses did (Exodus 33:11). As I do, may I reflect your glory and be transformed into your likeness.

What Do You Believe?

Against all hope, Abraham in hope believed.
—ROMANS 4:18

It is one thing to say we believe there is a God. Many people believe God exists. But what do we believe *about* God? Do we believe, for instance, that He is powerful? Or are we inclined to think of Him as a figurehead, sitting on a heavenly throne while everything rages out of control "down here"?

Isaiah believed that God is the "Creator of the heavens, who stretches them out, who spreads out the earth with all that springs from it, who gives breath to its people, and life to those who walk on it" (Isaiah 42:5). Such a God exercises unmatched authority and power over every aspect of life. Honestly, I cannot wrap my mind around such power. But with faith, I can let God's power wrap itself around my mind.

Perhaps that is what Abraham did when he chose to believe "against all hope." Romans 8:21 tells us he was "fully persuaded that God had power to do what he had promised."

Lord, give me faith like Abraham's. Help me lean on you in confidence that you have the power to do what you promise.

How's Your Signal?

Come near to God
and he will come near to you.
—JAMES 4:8

My cell phone taught me an important life lesson one weekend. We were relaxing at the lake, one of my favorite places on earth. But I wasn't so happy about our idyllic location that day. Instead I was seething with impatience. I couldn't get a cell signal. At first I blamed my phone. But then I realized my phone was dependable. It was the signal in the area that was not.

That's when I had my *aha* moment. God is always dependable. But I'm more like that signal—sometimes dependable but sometimes remote, inaccessible. I'm thankful God doesn't get impatient with me at such times. If He did, I'd be tempted to pull even further away from Him. Instead, I know I can move in close, strengthen the "signal" between us, and receive with joy the pleasure of His company.

Take time today to sit quietly, then journal what you hear God speaking to you.

Tree Talk

Just as you received Christ Jesus as Lord,
continue to live your lives in him, rooted and built up
in him, strengthened in the faith as you were taught,
and overflowing with thankfulness.

—COLOSSIANS 2:6–7

I love how Paul describes the progress of our faith in these verses. It begins when we *receive* a relationship with Christ Jesus. Once that relationship begins with our Savior and Lord, a lot happens!

We don't receive and then stop. We don't receive and then return to our old, independent ways. No, we *continue* to live *in* Him. *In* confidence in His power. *In* awareness of His presence. *In* imitation of His character.

As we continue in Him, two things happen. First, we *put down roots*, like a tree. We go deeper into the rich soil of Christ, drawing from Him everything we need to sustain life. Those roots nourish us and stabilize us. And second, we are *built up*. Again, like a tree, as our roots go deeper, our branches strengthen and spread and bear fruit. We become trees of life where others come to discover the appeal of life with Christ.

Pour yourself a glass of lemonade today. Find a big old shade tree to sit under. Then spend some time talking with God about how you can become more treelike.

Two Truths

I have no greater joy than to hear that
my children are walking in the truth.
—3 JOHN 1:4

The truth we see when we look at ourselves is not often the same truth God sees when He looks at us. Our "truth" limits us; God's truth opens doors.

The "truth" about Joseph is that he was a spoiled-brat-turned-slave and ex-con. God's truth: Joseph was the perfect instrument to save his family, the ancestors of Christ.

The "truth" about Rahab is that she was a prostitute. God's truth: Rahab would play a pivotal role in helping the Israelites take the Promised Land.

The "truth" about Esther is that she was a slave girl married to a Gentile. God's truth: Esther alone could save His people from an impending massacre.

The "truth" about Mary is that she was an unmarried peasant girl. God's truth: Mary was His choice to be the mother of Jesus.

Somewhere in their life journeys, you can bet the enemy stepped in with the lie that each of these people was too imperfect for God to use. But the evidence tells us they all rejected the lie and let God work out His truth in their lives.

What "truth" are you telling yourself that is holding you back from God's plans and purposes for your life? What door-opening truth do you think He is trying to tell you?

Multiple Choice

Choose life.
—DEUTERONOMY 30:19

When I first read this directive in Deuteronomy 30:19, I snickered. Who wouldn't choose life? I was only thinking of one alternative to choosing life: choosing death. I wasn't considering that I could choose a life that was different from the one I was living.

You see, Jesus says, "The thief comes only to steal and kill and destroy; I have come that they may have life, and have it to the full" (John 10:10). In other words, He came not only to give us life but to give us *abundant* life. Not just existence, just getting by, just one more day at the office. No, He offers a life of abundance. And this left me wondering, *Am I choosing abundant life today?*

Picture this day as having two handles: the handle of fear and the handle of faith. Now, divide a sheet of paper into two columns. Imagine one column is the handle of fear, and list the fears and worries that are weighing you down right now, keeping you from choosing an abundant life. Imagine the other column is the handle of faith. List some of the truths you have been learning about God and His promises from your devotional times, your conversations with friends of faith, your Bible reading, and so on. Which handle will you choose today?

HALT

Do you not know that your bodies are the temple
of the Holy Spirit, who is in you, whom you
have received from God?

—1 CORINTHIANS 6:19

These devotionals may be spiritual in focus, but we need to take care of ourselves physically and mentally as well. HALT is an acrostic many counselors use to represent four areas in which we should continuously examine ourselves to stay physically and mentally strong. H stands for hungry, A stands for angry, L for lonely, and T for tired.

I encourage you to evaluate how you are doing today, using the following questions:

Hungry. Are you eating well? Is your body being supplied with the nutrients it needs to function at its best?

Angry. How about tension? Are you easily angered? Are you sleeping, exercising, doing what's needed to keep stress levels down and happy hormones up?

Lonely. Are you taking time for those friendships we have talked so much about?

Tired. How tired are you? Are you sleeping? So often things look much different after a good night's rest.

Don't be fooled into equating busyness with godliness. Stop at times and allow physical rest for your body.

Using the HALT acrostic, identify a few ways you can take better care of yourself.

Never in Vain

Let us not become weary in doing good.
—GALATIANS 6:9

Our culture measures success by big, noticeable results and the attention they bring. But our individual spiritual efforts usually remain a small, anonymous part of a much greater whole. You may recall that according to 1 Corinthians 3:6, one of us may plant a seed, someone else may water it, but ultimately it's God who brings growth from what we've done.

Sometimes I get discouraged that I'm not "seeing" the fruit of my labor. Are the kids heeding my advice? Are my ways of sharing my faith being noticed? Is God using anything I do to bring about anything good? Focusing on visible, measurable success brings weariness. But focusing on being faithful frees us from weariness and helps us stay steadfast to God's purposes.

What are some ways others have done good to you through small, barely noticeable actions? Remember how much that meant to you the next time you are tempted to value big results over steady service.

A Fresh Perspective

For as [a man] thinks in his heart, so he is.

—PROVERBS 23:7 NKJV

What you believe really does matter. When you believe you are a failure, you will see every aspect of your life as a failure. When you believe your life will never change, you doom yourself to the status quo. When you believe mediocrity is the best you can do, you'll live a just-get-by existence instead of discovering your potential.

God doesn't always look at your life the same way you do. You may see failure, but He sees fresh starts. You may see mediocrity, but He sees strength.

What is one area of your life that you want to look at from God's perspective today instead of your own?

Without Words

> I have calmed and quieted myself ...
> like a weaned child with its mother.
>
> —PSALM 131:2

When I talk about spending time with God, do you get nervous because you don't know what you would say to Him? Let me suggest another way of thinking about this important part of your life.

A small child can spend all day in her mother's presence with very little actual conversation. The mother may be busy at her desk or in the kitchen or laundry room. The child may be absorbed with a doll or building blocks. Yet they are still spending time together. The child knows her mother is present, and the mother knows her child is fine.

And what about that friend you take road trips with? Do you chatter the entire time, or do you have long spells where you are aware of each other, happy to be sitting next to each other, but silent—just taking in the scenery?

Sometimes spending time with God means going through our day with awareness of His nearness, without the need for words. It can be the simple companionship of that mother and child, or the two friends in the car. Doesn't that sound inviting?

Spend some time in God's presence today, with the quiet contentment of a little child. Then journal about your experience.

Crazy Little Interruptions

The end of a matter is better than its beginning.
—ECCLESIASTES 7:8

Some things do need to be said more than once, but nothing needs to be said 248 times. Yet one day I sent the same e-mail not once but 248 times!

That day started as any other, but by 8:00 a.m. I knew something had gone terribly wrong. My cell phone lit up. Our 800 line was ringing nonstop. Emails poured in. "What's going on?" people wanted to know. "Stop the e-mail!"

Little did I know we had seventeen hours to endure the computer glitch. I started out calm but turned frantic as the calls persisted. What a helpless feeling knowing that people across the United States were getting the same e-mail from me not randomly, or even hourly, but every five minutes!

Hesitantly, I returned calls to women I'd never met. And that's when a crazy day became one of the best days I've had in a while. I met, by phone, the nicest, most understanding women. No one greeted me with anything other than kindness, and by the end of the day, I could giggle with a friend at the craziness of it all.

When life is interrupted by the unexpected and unusual, it reassures us we're not alone.

Besides God, who's got your back when life gets a little crazy?

If I Were You

"Praise be to the Lord, ... because he has come
to his people and redeemed them."
—LUKE 1:68

My oldest son, Trey, was on the way to a career in pro baseball. Then with one snap, his chance was gone. I walked with him through disappointment, surgeries, tears, all the while stuffing my own ragged emotions. A couple years later, I decided to write God a letter:

God, if I had been you, I would have thought long and hard before taking away Trey's chances at baseball. If I were you, I would have honored the little boy who wore the Scripture on his cap ... who tirelessly worked, yet gave you all the credit ... who was noted for carrying the cross in his pocket. If I were you, God, I would have ...

"I hear you, Kim," He replied. "But if you had been me, would you have given your son to a hurting and dying world? *Because that is what I did.*"

Through Jesus' death and resurrection, God still breaks through our losses today and brings healing and new life. Take hope in that great truth. Let it comfort you despite the losses you may be carrying. God redeems everything.

Are you angry about a situation beyond your control? If so, tell God how unfair it feels. Then give it to Him.

Do I Dare Hope?

"So keep up your courage … for I have faith in God
that it will happen just as he told me."

—ACTS 27:25

A mom I know has discovered—as many parents do—that
our faith does not always ensure our children's faith. She
and her husband have suffered lots of hurt and disappointment because of their young adult's decisions.

Recently, however, there have been signs of a break-
through. The mom is both thrilled and scared. "Do I dare
hope that she is coming around?" she asked me. "Do I dare
hope that my prayers are about to be answered?"

When we're in despair, we're afraid to allow ourselves
another glimmer of hope—we've been on that emotional
rollercoaster before. Many of you know exactly what I'm
talking about. At such times, I often think of Abraham in
Romans 4:18: "Against all hope, Abraham in hope believed."
Even when Abraham *had* no hope, he *believed* in hope. Or
you might say that even when Abraham had no hope he
hoped in the reliability of God's promises.

*What is the basis of your hope today? If it is faith in God,
then, yes, we can encourage one another to dare to hope and
never give up.*

Roar Back

Your enemy the devil prowls around like a roaring lion
looking for someone to devour.

—1 PETER 5:8

I have witnessed repeatedly Satan's two most common tricks: He roars with the voice of discouragement—and with the voice of doubt. I've let the enemy's roar drive me to anorexia, anxiety attacks, and depression. His roars have sent me into a spiral of performing, conforming, and doubting myself. As someone who has been there, may I encourage you: Don't give up. Don't retreat. ROAR back!

Realize that all your enemy can do is roar. He'll make a lot of noise, but that's all he's got. *Observe* your situation. To which of the enemy's lies are you most vulnerable? *Apply* God's truths. Once you discern the lies, you can roar back with specific spiritual truths. *Respond* with the confidence that comes from belonging to the Maker of heaven and earth.

In Luke 10:17–19, Jesus' disciples "returned with joy and said, 'Lord, even the demons submit to us in your name.' He replied, 'I saw Satan fall like lightning from heaven. I have given you authority to … overcome all the power of the enemy; nothing will harm you'" (vv. 17–19). Does that put Satan's power into perspective for you?

God, I praise you today that, in your power, I can roar back at the enemy.

Expert Advice

You discern my going out and my lying down;
you are familiar with all my ways.

—PSALM 139:3

My firstborn, Trey, was a colicky little guy. *Oh my!* I kept thinking. *I'm his mom. Surely I should be able to do something.* But it just went on and on.

Finally I went to the doctor—the expert—and I said, "I don't know what to do. He cries around the clock. My husband travels. I've got to get some rest. I don't know what to do. Tell me what to do. I've got to get some rest." And this expert said, "Well, it's very easy. You're either feeding him too much, or you're not feeding him enough." *Seriously, doctor,* I thought, *is that the best an expert can do?*

Basically he was saying, "You've got to know your child. You've got to listen and distinguish between the different cries. You've got to figure out your own child, because you're the one with a *relationship* with that child."

*Do you see any principles here for how God relates to you?
How you relate to God?*

Sweet Sleep

If our hearts condemn us, we know that God is greater
than our hearts, and he knows everything.

—1 JOHN 3:20

It gets late. Life slows down. And your mind begins to go over every part of your day. Rarely are you completely satisfied with your actions, and so guilt seeps in. And with the guilt comes sleeplessness. Sound familiar?

God wants you to know one thing: He is greater than any guilt or regret. God may see where you could have done better, but He sees much more. He sees your desire to know and love Him, and He says, "Don't condemn yourself! I know all there is to know about you, and I love you. You are mine."

Tonight, empty your mind and heart of regret. Sleep guilt-free, my friend. Your God is great!

Disqualified?

"You are right when you say you have no husband.
The fact is, you have had five."
—JOHN 4:17–18

Are you running from your past? Do you pray no one finds out about your mistakes? Do you hold back from opportunities because you believe your past disqualifies you?

When Jesus questioned the Samaritan woman, His intent was not to humiliate her. Rather, He knew she could only grasp the depth of His unconditional love if she first acknowledged the depth of her sin. The moment she faced the truth about herself and the truth about Christ's love, transformation happened. She no longer let the person she once was control the woman she was becoming. And what happened next? "Many more became believers" because of Jesus' words (v. 41).

Something similar happened with the woman caught in adultery. "Jesus … asked her, 'Woman, where are they? Has no one condemned you?' 'No one, sir,' she said. 'Then neither do I condemn you,' Jesus declared. 'Go now and leave your life of sin'" (John 8:10–11).

God of grace, guide me into a deeper understanding of your perfect love, so I can face the truth about my imperfect past. I release it to you today.

When the Battles Keep Coming

"The battle is not yours, but God's."
—2 CHRONICLES 20:15

We often read the story of Joshua conquering Jericho with a sigh of relief. He faced a battle, and with God's help he won the battle in the end. But do you know that Joshua faced dozens of battles after that one? Jericho may be the battle he is famous for, but it is certainly not his only one. His life was a series of battles against a series of enemies. The outcomes were not always the same. But one thing remained the same: God was with Him.

Likewise, we will always face battles, large and small. But don't think that because you're battling, you're not where God wants you to be. You're most likely doing exactly what God wants you to do, exactly where He wants you to do it. And He is in the battle with you. In every battle life brings to you, rest assured that God has your back.

Talk with God about the battle you're facing today. Be honest about your fears and frustrations. But also be thankful that He is in the battle with you. In fact, He has made your battle His battle. You do not fight alone!

Anxiety-Free

Do not be anxious about anything,
but in every situation, by prayer and petition,
with thanksgiving, present your requests to God.
And the peace of God, which transcends all understanding,
will guard your hearts and your minds in Christ Jesus.

—PHILIPPIANS 4:6–7

Don't be anxious? Really, Paul? What about the morning news? Not to mention our personal worries about health, job security, kids going off to college.

Paul kindly gives us the equation to the impossible:

Worry about Nothing + Pray about Everything = God's Peace.

God doesn't condemn your worrying; He understands you will be anxious. Even more, He can use your fears to make you stronger. The path to that strength is prayer.

Here are some words to get your prayer started: "Dear Father, when I get anxious, I feel trapped, unable to think about anything but my fears. Yet here you are, showing me the path to freedom from anxiety. I want to follow you on that path, and so I will begin as the verse tells me to—by talking to you about what worries me. Here goes …"

Who Gets the First Word?

The Sovereign Lord has given me a well-instructed
tongue. … He wakens me morning by morning,
wakens my ear to listen like one being instructed.

—ISAIAH 50:4

Have you ever heard someone describe a time she was struggling, then end her account something like this: "Kelly knew just what to say"? I walk away thinking, *I want to be like Kelly.* The good news is, I can. And so can you. How? By listening to God morning by morning by morning.

Getting a "well-instructed tongue" is not about being smarter, or getting more experience under our belts, or memorizing the entire Bible. It's about starting the day listening to God speak to you through His Word (not the TV news, and not those snarky posts that show up on Facebook sometimes, and not the gossipy coworker who greets you at the coffee machine).

If that sounds undoable, here's the part I *really* love: He will wake you up every morning to be with Him! "Kelly" takes God up on His offer every morning. As a result, her words are full of wisdom and healing.

How much time are you spending in God's Word? Starting today, try following in Kelly's footsteps by letting God speak to you daily through His written Word.

July

Doing the Right Thing

> The sinful nature wants to do evil, which is just the oppo-
> site of what the Spirit wants. ... These two forces
> are constantly fighting each other,
> so you are not free to carry out your good intentions.
> —GALATIANS 5:17 NLT

"Why should I be friendly toward a coworker who is gossiping about me? Isn't that hypocritical?" You might have a slightly different version of this question, but whatever the version, the answer is the same. Absolutely not!

Many times you will want to lash out at someone. But when you choose to grit your teeth or bite your tongue and smile, that's good, not hypocritical! Sure, you'd like your emotions to match your actions, but when they don't you can still choose to do the right thing. Right actions lead to right feelings. It's never hypocritical to choose obedience to Christ over following your not-always-reliable emotions.

Fill me with you Spirit, Lord. I want to be a person who carries kindness and respect wherever I go, no matter what my "mood of the moment" might be.

To the Giver's Glory

Every good and perfect gift is from above,
coming down from the Father.
—JAMES 1:17

With no rain forecasted, Lee and I planned a trip to the beach. And guess what happened? Down came the rain! Yet we felt a strange pull to stay the course. So, off we went. Seven hours later, with no end of the rain and backed-up traffic in sight, we decided to give up and turn around. Unknown to us, we stopped at just the right place to meet members of the Virginia Fire 13U baseball team.

"Ma'am, would you like to buy some donuts?" asked a young lad. His team was raising funds to attend a tournament. I handed over what little cash I had. What happened next transformed an ordinary encounter into the extraordinary.

My contribution was neither the team's first nor their largest, but you would have thought I had given the moon. Thankfulness beamed from this little guy's eyes. He grinned and gave me a big thumbs-up. "We're gonna win just for you!" he declared.

The giver of so little, I had been given so much. Driving home that day, I was reminded of all the gifts I receive daily. This little team had motivated me to exhibit their "glory to God" kind of thankfulness.

What are you thankful for today? Make a list. Then send a handwritten thank-you to the people you appreciate the most.

Relationally Speaking

[It is God] who created the heavens
and stretched them out, who spread forth
the earth and that which comes from it.
—ISAIAH 42:5 NKJV

One day last summer, as I came around the corner from my daily run, the sight of full-bloom crepe myrtles took my breath away. When we first planted them in our yard, I feared that the scrawny limbs would not live. I never dreamed they would burst forth with such an abundance of beauty.

That's our God, I thought. With just a word from Him all things were created (including crepe myrtles), and with His word the impossible is made possible.

For so many years, the second part of that truth confused me more than comforted me. If with one word God could prevent all these hurts, heal all pain and injustice, why would He not do that? It took a long while, but I finally realized that with God, it's more relational than situational.

God tucks relational opportunities amid each day's "impossible" situations. With whom have you bonded, for instance, because of your disagreeable circumstances? Ask God to open your eyes to see His relational purposes in each circumstance.

Freedom to Choose

"Choose for yourselves this day whom you will serve."
—JOSHUA 24:15

We celebrate our national freedom every year. But how often do we celebrate our personal freedom?

While there's always more work to be done (because we are all works in progress), we can still celebrate each small step we take toward mental, emotional, relational, financial, or spiritual freedom.

I'm convinced that a life of freedom is built from "ordinary" everyday choices more than from major decisions. For example, today we can choose good over evil (Psalm 34:14). Obedience over foolishness (Proverbs 10:8). Honesty over deceit (Colossians 3:9). We make hundreds of daily choices, and they become the cobblestones that create our path to freedom.

So keep making those godly, freeing choices. And bring on the fireworks!

At the end of the day, look back and identify the freeing choices you made today with God's help.

Seven Simple Words

"But because you say so, I will."
—LUKE 5:5

Peter had fished all night but hadn't caught a thing. He was exhausted. Empty-handed. Embarrassed. Yet just as Peter was rolling up his nets, Jesus came along and said, "Put out into deep water, and let down the nets for a catch" (v. 4). Can you picture Peter rolling his eyes?

Peter might have rolled his eyes, but his words revealed his heart: "But because you say so, I will." Seven simple words.

What does Christ mean when He tells you to go into deeper water? He is talking about resolve, not giving up even when all seems lost. He is talking about focus, not on how people are reacting but rather on what God is asking. He is urging you to go beyond your feelings, talents, and resources to stand on what you know God has promised, and what only His power at work in you can do. He is talking about looking beyond the obvious to see things yet to be seen—that God is working and, at just the right moment, your obedience will be rewarded infinitely more than you could have imagined.

Do you dare echo Peter's seven simple words? They changed his life. They will change your life too.

Of Two Minds

Do not conform to the pattern of this world,
but be transformed by the renewing of your mind.

—ROMANS 12:2

Let's talk about two ways the minds of believers conform to the pattern of this world.

We settle for the world's truth and fail to complete it with God's truth. We try the world's offerings—material belongings, titles, status—thinking they'll make us feel complete. But instead, we end up with debt, food addictions, alcoholism, worry, and feelings of inferiority, discouragement, and depression. We know something is missing. We know there has to be something more. Or …

We profess God's truths but never acknowledge ours. This is what I did. I could recite biblical principles, but I wasn't willing to acknowledge the truth about myself. It was far more important to me to masquerade a near-perfect life. Yet daily, yearly, I was paying the price, for without being honest about my pain, I couldn't become what God wanted me to become.

Which of these patterns of thinking rings true for you? Maybe both do. Invite God today to show you where your thinking needs to be renewed.

Country Music and God's Will

With what shall I come before the Lord and bow down
before the exalted God? Shall I come before him
with burnt offerings, with … rivers of olive oil?
Shall I offer my firstborn … the fruit of my body?

—MICAH 6:6–7

Micah was one of the first to unmask his frustration about figuring out God's will. He wondered, *How much will I have to sacrifice to be accepted by God? What will I have to give up?* Then he listed some of the things that meant the most to him—things he enjoyed, loved, or that brought him security.

Do you ask questions like Micah's? I sure did! For instance:

- Can I be in God's will and still like country music?
- Is it OK if I don't know where Micah is in the Bible?
- Can I wear cute clothes and be in God's will?
- Do I have to quote Scripture in public to please God?

You might be laughing right now, but be honest! What's on your list? What do you think you may have to sacrifice as you contemplate God's will for your life?

Micah's conclusion is a gift to us all: "What does the LORD require of you? To act justly and to love mercy and to walk humbly with your God" (v. 8). How freeing to realize God is not interested in *what* we have to offer. His sole interest is in the worshiper! You. And me.

What was on your list of sacrifices you thought were necessary to please God? How has this passage from Micah changed your list?

Enjoy the Walk

"I will walk with you."
—LEVITICUS 26:12

On our quest to discover God's will, we're not likely to encounter a road sign that says, *Welcome, you have arrived at God's will.* So if we're not looking for a sign, what *are* we looking for?

Among my favorite memories of my granddad are my walks with him. Granddad would always extend his hand and invite me to walk to Top Street with him, our favorite destination in our Virginia town. I vividly recall how safe I felt as I tucked my tiny hand into his big one.

Our part in finding God's will is simply saying yes to the invitation to walk with God daily. I say yes by beginning my day with some type of devotional time. This helps me to stay more focused on saying yes throughout the day to His invitations: to call a friend and encourage her, or to be patient with the rude store clerk. We can count on the invitations; our part is to be present (and alert) right where we are—in our kitchen, at work, running errands—and to say yes.

Think of following God's will as I do: taking His hand for the day and paying attention to where He takes you. And don't forget to enjoy the walk!

Today I say yes to you, God.

Out of the Cocoon

We all, who with unveiled faces contemplate
the Lord's glory, are being transformed into his image
with ever-increasing glory, which comes from the Lord,
who is the Spirit.

—2 CORINTHIANS 3:18

God's goal for us is that we be transformed—that we experience a change on the inside that brings about a change on the outside. The butterfly is a great illustration of this in nature. It starts out as an ugly caterpillar that over time is transformed into a majestic butterfly—something completely new—because of what goes on *inside* the cocoon.

As we seek God, as we focus more on Him, we experience a growing desire to be more like Him. We experience a metamorphosis from doing what we want to what God wants.

God's will is not concealed from us. When we understand God's will from this perspective, we are freed from the anxiety of missing God's will *today* and can rest in the cocoon of His love, knowing we will emerge as butterflies in His timing.

In the song "Diamonds" Hawk Nelson describes how the joy of the Lord is our strength, how He turns dust into diamonds. God works in and through you to change you from something ordinary into someone beautiful. Thank Him for your transformation today.

I'm the Best!

For as he thinks in his heart, so is he.

—PROVERBS 23:7 NKJV

A little boy went out to the backyard to play with a bat and baseball. He said to himself, "I am the best hitter in the world." Then he threw the ball up in the air, took a swing at it, and missed.

Without a moment's hesitation, he tossed it in the air again, saying as he swung the bat, "I'm the best hitter in the world." Again he missed. Strike two.

He tossed the ball a third time, even more determined, saying, "I am the best hitter in the world!" But he missed again. Strike three.

The boy set down his bat with the biggest smile ever. "Well, what do you know," he said, "I'm the best *pitcher* in the world!"

What we believe, we receive.

Take whatever comes your way today, and rather than expecting the same-old-same-old, take charge by expecting more. Then make your actions match your expectations. Do what a winner would do. Begin living as if the "infinitely more" of Ephesians 3:20 has already happened.

Hope Givers

> "I know that you can do all things;
> no purpose of yours can be thwarted."
>
> —JOB 42:2

Job, a man besieged by troubles and trials, made this astonishing declaration to God in the midst of his suffering (*in the midst of it*—not after everything was resolved).

Everyone is dealing with hard stuff. Everyone. Everyone needs someone to believe in, someone who can handle the personal worries and the big "what's this world coming to?" worries. God is that someone.

You know it in your head and heart. But when hope is in short supply, do you send a different message?

Be like Job today. In the midst of your trials, announce the truth about God. He can do anything. No purpose of His can be thwarted. Be a hope giver.

Called to Encourage

"Simon, Simon! Indeed, Satan has asked for you,
that he may sift you as wheat. But I have prayed for you,
that your faith should not fail; and when you have
returned to Me, strengthen your brethren."

—LUKE 22:31–32 NKJV

As Jesus faced death, He pulled Peter aside to strengthen and prepare him for what was about to happen. Jesus knew that Peter's loyalty would be severely tested, so He expressed His confidence that even though Peter's faith would falter, it would not be fatal. Peter's mistakes would make him stronger and equip him to strengthen others.

No matter how busy your life is, strengthening others for their journeys is one of the most important ministries you could practice. Ask God to show you how you can strengthen one person today: through a note or e-mail, a phone call, a small gift, or some gesture you'd never have thought of on your own. Then thank God for allowing you to share in His ministry of encouragement and support.

Slow to Speak

My dear brothers and sisters, take note of this:
Everyone should be quick to listen, slow to speak
and slow to become angry.

—JAMES 1:19

I really messed up yesterday. Do you have days like that? I bet we all do. The truth is, we are not perfect; at times we just don't measure up. One way we become blessings is when we allow those around us the freedom to talk about their feelings of failure and falling short.

So keep your eyes open. You may meet someone today who needs a compassionate, nonjudgmental listener. Rather than offering advice or pointing out a "fix," simply listen.

While you're looking for ways to be "quick to listen" with others, make sure you have a good listener or two or three in your life.

The Pleasure of Your Company

Whether you turn to the right or to the left,
your ears will hear a voice behind you, saying,
"This is the way; walk in it!"

—ISAIAH 30:21

You don't have to beg God to show up each day. You don't need the perfect chair to pray in or the perfect Bible translation. He is always ready to spend time with you. He loves the sound of your voice. As you set aside some time each day to talk to God and listen to Him, He will become real to you as never before.

But don't forget that He is also at your side as you run errands, shovel snow, sit in that board meeting, or attend your Pilates class. You can keep your conversation with Him going all day!

Father, thank you for wanting my company—all day, every day.

No Quitting

Therefore we do not lose heart. ... Our light and
momentary troubles are achieving for us an eternal glory.
... What is seen is temporary, but what is unseen is eternal.
—2 CORINTHIANS 4:16–18

Don't quit! That's the message in this passage. As easy as it
would be to throw up your hands in surrender and walk
away from that difficult relationship, those financial woes,
that overwhelming task, that health challenge ... God's
Word counsels you to keep on keeping on.

Whatever you are facing today, draw upon the strength
of the Holy Spirit through prayer, and then press on. Don't
forsake tomorrow's blessings by giving up today.

*Help me, Lord, to fix my eyes "not on what is seen, but on
what is unseen, since what is seen is temporary, but what is
unseen is eternal" (v. 18).*

I'm No Bad Girl!

A good name is more desirable than great riches;
to be esteemed is better than silver or gold.

—PROVERBS 22:1

A couple had two little boys, ages eight and ten, who were excessively mischievous. If any shenanigans occurred in their town, their two young sons were usually involved.

The parents had heard that a new pastor in town had been successful in disciplining children, so they decided to ask him to speak to their boys. The pastor agreed, but asked to see the boys individually. The eight-year-old went first.

The pastor sat the boy down and asked sternly, "Where is God?" The boy made no response, so the pastor repeated even more sternly, "Where is God?" Again the boy was silent. The pastor raised his voice even more and shook his finger in the boy's face. "Where … is … God?"

The boy bolted from the room, ran home, and hid in the closet. His older brother followed him and asked what had happened. The younger brother replied, "We are in really big trouble this time. God is missing, and they think we did it."

How can you be the kind of woman people think of first when something good happens, not when something bad happens?

One Mind, One Voice

> May the God who gives endurance and encouragement
> give you the same attitude of mind toward each other that
> Christ Jesus had, so that with one mind and one voice you
> may glorify the God and Father of our Lord Jesus Christ.
>
> —ROMANS 15:5–6

When I read these words of Paul, I knew what I wanted to do: encourage all of you to join me with one mind and one voice in giving glory to God today.

Are you with me?

Let's start by making two lists. First, make a list of the reasons you love God. For instance, you might love God for His patience or His creativity or His unending love.

Next, make a list of things you want to thank Him for today. This list will focus on what you have received from God: your children, enough income to make another mortgage payment, or good health.

Making those lists gets us all to the "one mind" part of Paul's prayer. Now, let's read our lists aloud to God—in "one voice." Yes, we are in different locations and time zones, but I believe God will hear our praises and thanksgiving as intended—a single, unified voice lifted to Him in love.

Now that you've tried this once, share the experience. Invite friends near and far to join you with many lists but one voice.

100 Percent Wax-Free

This I pray, that your love may abound still more and more
in knowledge and all discernment, that you may approve
the things that are excellent, that you may be sincere
and without offense till the day of Christ.

—PHILIPPIANS 1:9–10 NKJV

According to one popular legend, the word *sincere* that
Paul used in this verse is derived from the Latin *sine*
(without) and *cera* (wax). Dishonest sculptors in ancient
Rome and Greece covered flaws in their work with wax to
deceive the buyer. Therefore, a sculpture "without wax" was
honest in its perfection. It would not melt and change shape
in the hot Mediterranean sun

When Paul prayed for "wax-free" believers, he was praying for people to be real inside and outside, in good times and
in times when the heat went up. Let's pray the same for each
other.

*In "What If We Were Real" former American Idol contestant
and Grammy nominee Mandisa sings about sharing her
brokenness with others. Check out the lyrics today.*

Beauty from Ashes

He has made everything beautiful in its time.

—ECCLESIASTES 3:11

This verse in Ecclesiastes becomes our hope: The best is yet to come. God's blessings are on their way! And this becomes our challenge: We can't give up.

In Isaiah 61:1–3, the prophet Isaiah describes the ministry of the coming Messiah: "The LORD has anointed me to proclaim good news to the poor. He has sent me to bind up the brokenhearted, to proclaim freedom for the captives and release from darkness for the prisoners, to proclaim the year of the LORD's favor and the day of vengeance of our God, to comfort all who mourn, and provide for those who grieve in Zion—to bestow on them a crown of beauty instead of ashes, the oil of joy instead of mourning, and a garment of praise instead of a spirit of despair" (Isaiah 61:1–3).

A crown of beauty instead of ashes. Did you get that? God will make everything beautiful. In His time. In His way. Even the ashes of our lives with become beautiful.

What ugly burden in your life do you want to see made beautiful? Give that burden to God. Tell Him how tired you are of carrying it and hiding it from others. But also tell Him of your determination to believe that your burdens are becoming beautiful, because He said it is so.

God, Where Are You?

"The LORD himself goes before you and will be with you;
he will never leave you nor forsake you."

—DEUTERONOMY 31:8

I cannot name all the times I have asked God, "Where are you?" Definitely when my youngest was deathly ill. And when my oldest suffered a career-ending injury. And yes, when a move was ending life as we had always known it.

What has caused you to ask this question?

I'm far from triumphant over the temptation to doubt God's presence, but I have found that prayer helps to remind me that He is always present. He is committed to us. No matter had hard life gets, and how much we may not understand, He has promised never to leave or forsake us.

Prayer changes the cry of my heart from "Where are You, God?" to "There you are, God!"

"Where can I go from your Spirit? Where can I flee from your presence? If I go up to the heavens, you are there; if I make my bed in the depths, you are there" (Psalm 139:7–8). How do these words of the psalmist inspire you?

Already Queens

Before a young woman's turn came to go to King Xerxes,
she had to complete twelve months of beauty treatments.

—ESTHER 2:12

Before becoming queen, Esther spent a year just preparing to enter the king's presence and *maybe* be approved by him. A whole group of would-be queens endured "the twelve months of prescribed beauty treatments—six months' treatment with oil of myrrh followed by six months with perfumes and various cosmetics" after which each girl went in to see King Xerxes (Esther 2:12 MSG).

We don't have to do that with our King. We don't prepare ourselves daily for approval. We are already accepted. We are already chosen. We are already loved. We prepare our hearts daily for service. That's a *big* difference!

How does this assurance of God's approval change your preparation for the day ahead?

Dream a Little Dream

> From him and through him
> and for him are all things.
> —ROMANS 11:36

If, within the next few days, you were granted the power to buy your dream, what would that dream be? If you were given a magic wand to wave over your circumstances, how would things change? Perhaps you would magically mend a relationship. Or buy healing of the emotional pain you carry that no one else can see. Maybe you want an end to the anger you feel toward God. Would your magic wand have you obtaining a more satisfying job? Getting into your dream home? Maybe your dream wouldn't be about you at all; maybe you long to see someone you love realize his or her dream.

For anything you can dream this morning, God says He has "infinitely more" than you could ever imagine (Ephesians 3:20). So don't think that just because you're not off to that new job, or you still can't afford your dream house, that God has let you down. He's at work at this very moment doing something greater than the obvious, greater than you expect.

What might your life look like if you dared to believe your dream could come true?

Drinking Sand

"Come, all you who are thirsty, come to the waters."
—ISAIAH 55:1

One of my favorite movies is *The American President*. One moment rings in my ears every time I watch it.

One of the president's colleagues is trying to get him to be more assertive in his run for president. He says, "Mr. President, they [the American people] want leadership; they want truth. They just want truth." And he continues: "They're so thirsty for truth that they'll crawl through a desert toward a mirage, and when they discover there's no water, they'll drink the sand."

I can't get that image out of my head: how we can get so thirsty for the truth that when we can't find it, we're willing to drink whatever is there, even if it's sand.

Do you know anyone so thirsty she is drinking sand? Offer that person a cool cup of God's life-giving truth today.

Fear Says ...

"Seek first his kingdom and his righteousness, and all these
things will be given to you as well."
—MATTHEW 6:33

Have you heard the voice of fear lately? This is what it often sounds like:

- That can't be!
- I'm not qualified.
- I don't have time.
- That's not a good fit for my personality.
- I can't afford to do that!
- I wasn't expecting this!

The Sermon on the Mount contains God's answer to that voice of fear.

Start to memorize Matthew 6:33 today, and you will be on your way to replacing fear with faith.

Running in the Right Direction

I run in the path of your commands,
for you have broadened my understanding.

—PSALM 119:32

When we're first getting acquainted with God's Word, we tend to run to it at "panic points"—when we face problems and challenges. We look for quick answers and fixes. And you know what, that's OK. The point is, we are running to the Word and not to our former, less reliable sources of wisdom.

Over time, though, His words become a part of who we are. We discover how active God's Word is, how transforming. We run to our daily visits with God through His Word with great expectations. We know we will meet Him there. We know He will replace the panic and pressure of our daily lives with peace. The more time we spend with the Source of wisdom, the more His wisdom becomes ingrained in us, broadening our understanding of life, equipping us for abundant living.

How can you get better acquainted with God's Word? What is one practical step you need to take? If you don't know where to begin, ask for help from a friend whose life demonstrates a love for the Bible.

True Life

So I will always remind you of these things,
even though you know them and are firmly
established in the truth you now have.

—2 PETER 1:12

Over the years, five core truths have shaped my life:

1. I was planned, handmade, and labeled very good
   (Psalm 139:13–16; Genesis 1:31).
2. I was created with a unique plan and purpose and
   given everything I need to accomplish that plan (Jeremiah 29:11; 2 Timothy 3:17).
3. Mistakes, poor choices, and abuse cannot negate God's
   plan for my life. God can make all things work for my
   good and His glory (Romans 8:28; Genesis 50:20).
4. God presents me with small, daily opportunities
   to serve Him and others, and He empowers me to
   respond (Ephesians 2:10; Colossians 4:5).
5. God's desire for me is abundant life through His power
   at work in me beyond anything I could imagine (John
   10:10; Ephesians 3:20).

I pray that each day, you will add to the truths that shape
your life into the masterpiece God planned it to be.

*Which of the Scriptures above resonates with you the most?
Write it on a sticky note or index card, and place it somewhere
prominent, so you'll see it throughout your day.*

The Gift of a Friend

Your love has given me great joy and encouragement,
because you ... have refreshed the hearts
of the Lord's people.

—PHILEMON 1:7

As I lunched with a friend this week, I saw the pain on her face. She wondered aloud if she could ever believe again after all she was going through. Oh, the many times I have been where she is! I pray for my friend in this season of pain and trials, and I am confident that one day she will again marvel at the flawlessness of God's plan.

Through all my trials, I've learned God's will is different from mine but always executed perfectly. I've learned His timing is different from mine, but His promises are always delivered at just the right time. I've also learned that our feelings are not cause for regret or shame. Our feelings are to be felt. I've learned not to run from the emotion, but rather to sit in it for a while. By staying in the emotion and thinking about it, I can learn from it.

If the sad person you face is the one in the mirror, do what my friend did: Find someone you trust and share your heart and your raw feelings. In the midst of the pain, you'll discover something priceless—a friend who cares for you. Just where you are.

Pride Buster

Zacchaeus … wanted to see who Jesus was.

—LUKE 19:2–3

Zacchaeus had many reasons to be proud. His career was thriving: Not only was he a tax collector, which gave him a lot of power (unpopular power!), but he as a *chief* tax collector. He was wealthy. And he was resourceful: He might have been short, but he showed great cleverness in working around that liability.

Then he heard Jesus was coming to town. Was it mere curiosity that led him to climb a tree to get the best view of this visitor? Was it the first pang of spiritual hunger? We don't know, but we do know what happened next. Jesus saw him and said, "Come down immediately. I must stay at your house today" (v. 5).

Zacchaeus gave up his pride that day and a great deal of his wealth, but he gained much more. As Jesus declared, "Today salvation has come to this house."

A few words from Jesus were enough to make a prideful man drop out of a tree, giddy with excitement. What do you need to hear Him say to you today?

Well Preserved

"I will take hold of your hand. I will keep you."
—ISAIAH 42:6

'd like you to think about this: Whatever you are going through, whatever burdens you bear—and all of us bear burdens—God is not pacing the carpet of heaven wondering what to do next. He sees the load you carry, and He sees your pain and fear and sense of failure. But He sees something more. He sees how all these things are preparing you, are "making" you. And He is keeping you, preserving you even though life may at times seem crushing. Like a potter with clay, God's fingers are always on you, shaping you, making adjustments, forming you into something beautiful.

Check out the music video for "Beautiful Things" by Gungor and also by Shane & Shane. Both provide a visual and lyrical description of the way God transforms us in the midst of our pain.

More Than a Glance

Very early in the morning, while it was still dark,
Jesus got up, left the house and went off to a solitary place,
where he prayed.

—MARK 1:35

Of the four Gospels about Jesus, the shortest—Mark—is the most action packed. Again and again, Mark used the phrase "and immediately." Jesus immediately did this, then immediately did that, and so on. He preached, He taught, He healed, and then He did it some more. And He walked everywhere, while talking with His disciples and preparing them for their future ministries.

Yet I don't see a pressured Jesus, do you? He wasn't stressed out like we would be in His shoes, I mean, sandals. I believe the key is found in Mark 1:35. No matter what else was going on, He spent time daily focusing on His Father. Not *glancing* at His Father, but *focusing* on Him.

If Jesus needed that kind of time with God, how much more do we need it!

Susanna Wesley, the mother of many children, including John and Charles Wesley, found a clever way to spend time with God every day. When her children saw her sitting in the kitchen with her apron over her head, they knew she was praying and was not to be disturbed. Where is your "solitary place" of prayer?

Morning Hope

Because of the Lord's great love we are not consumed,
for his compassions never fail.
They are new every morning.
—LAMENTATIONS 3:22–23

I love the quietness of a new morning when the world still seems undisturbed and at peace. Yet in my mind's eye, I can see beyond the morning beauty and into the pain consuming many hearts and homes. The aftershock of hurtful words. Piles of bills. A devastating diagnosis. A broken relationship. Fruitless job searches.

What is trying to consume you today? Worry? An addiction? Regret? Loneliness? You can break free from this downward spiral by focusing on the truth of today's verse. Let it set you upon a landing place of hope.

Each day this week, before you get out of bed, thank God that His great love and compassion are new that morning.

August

The Hidden Arrow

We fix our eyes not on what is seen,
but on what is unseen.
—2 CORINTHIANS 4:18

The FedEx logo gives us a down-to-earth glimpse of what this verse is talking about. We've all seen the logo, right? But have you noticed the arrow in the logo? Most people don't, at first. But if you look closely between the "e" and the "x," you find the arrow.

Once you notice the arrow, your eyes are conditioned to go there every time. You can no longer not see it. It's the same with the people and circumstances we face each day. Hidden within every person, place, and circumstance are opportunities to join God in His ministry of healing and hope.

When we embrace this kingdom reality, we grow progressively sensitized to the multitudes that bump against us as we go about our daily routines. Our eyesight grows sharper, our hearing more acute. No longer do we sit in our corner and wonder when God will use us; now we see opportunities for good work everywhere we look. Welcome to the world of discernment.

What opportunities for service await you today? Ask God for eyes to see and ears to hear those who are hurting.

One Call Home

When I called, you answered me.
—PSALM 138:3

I got a call recently from my son. "Mom, I'm sorry I didn't call yesterday, but I had a really bad day."

"Are you OK now?"

"Well, I'm about to go into emergency surgery."

It only takes one phone call to turn your adult child into a little baby in your imagination. I didn't know what Austin was wearing, if he'd done his schoolwork, or if his bathroom was dirty. But none of it mattered. None of it affected how much I loved him and wanted to take care of him.

We may be grown up and accomplished. We may know how to dress for success and shine brightly in our social circles. God sees all that, and I believe He is proud of us, as any loving father would be. But when we hurt, we become God's little girls again. God doesn't hold back until we've accomplished our goals for the day and look our best. Instead, He rushes to us with His love and care.

By the way, my son had an appendectomy and was in class a day later. Medicine is full of wonders. But a God who rushes to the aid of His frightened child—that's an even greater wonder.

When I call on you, God, I know you'll come rushing to take care of me. What a wonder you are!

Trust Me

"Do not let your hearts be troubled."
—JOHN 14:1

As Jesus ministered in His unorthodox way, His disciples sometimes gave way to concern and discouragement. Thomas put words to this struggle to understand Jesus when he asked, "Lord, we don't know where you are going, so how can we know how to get there?"

As Jesus drew my attention to my masks and my burdens, I was wondering the same thing as Thomas: *Where are You going, Jesus, with all this garbage You are dredging up?* (Did He not understand I had spent a lifetime hiding this mess of heartbreak, shame, and regret?) *Now that You've dug it up, what do You want me to do with it? How do I even begin?*

Where I was going, I found out, was not as important as who I was going with. "Do not let your hearts be troubled" was Jesus' way of saying, "Trust Me, Kim. Will you just trust Me?"

"Trust me" is a lot to ask of someone whose trust had been shattered at age four. Jesus reassured me with these words: "I am the way and the truth and the life" (John 4:6).

What's troubling your heart today? How do Jesus' words reassure you?

The Sound of Silence

When I kept silent, my bones wasted away through my
groaning all day long.

—PSALM 32:3

We all carry around hurts, tragedies, disappointments, unfulfilled dreams, abuses, addictions, and more. Sure, we hide them. Or we try to pretty them up with our busy lives, shiny smiles, and peppy personalities. But no matter what we do, we know they are there.

Are you wasting away like the psalmist from keeping silent about the burdens in your life? He eventually told God about the pain and hurt he carried. And what did he receive from God? Unfailing love.

Read the rest of Psalm 32 in your Bible and then break your silence by talking to God, who is utterly trustworthy.

Willing Instruments

But you are a chosen people, a royal priesthood,
a holy nation, God's special possession,
that you may declare the praises of him who
called you out of darkness into his wonderful light.

—1 PETER 2:9

We are like ink pens; we are God's writing instruments. His eyes have rested upon us, He has chosen us, and His hand picks us up. He is the ink that flows through us. He uses our lives to write His message to others around us and to fulfill His purposes. Yet He never uses us without asking our permission. He seeks *willing* instruments. That's love, don't you think?

Consider the "Prayer of Saint Francis of Assisi," which begins: "Lord, make me an instrument of thy peace. Where there is hatred, let me sow love; where there is injury, pardon; where there is doubt, faith; where there is despair, hope; where there is darkness, light; where there is sadness, joy."

What story would you like God to write with your life?

View Changer

"You will grieve, but your grief will turn to joy."
—JOHN 16:20

When my mother died of cancer, I was convinced God had betrayed me by not answering my prayers for her healing. He took her from me just when she and I had reconciled after years of estrangement and were finally enjoying one another.

But God persisted in drawing near to me. And though I was struggling with this piece of my past, I persisted in spending time in His Word, seeking out His promises, getting His perspective. Gradually and steadily, my focus changed. I still wished Mother were just a phone call away. But I grew convinced that God intended to honor her—and use me—through both her life and death. That perspective began to motivate me to look forward, not backward, to embrace the opportunities He was about to set before me.

Is your view obstructed by the past? Or have you experienced the gift of a fresh perspective and clear outlook for the future? Ask God's help to keep your eyes on the hope that lies ahead.

Smell Like a Rose

Thanks be to God who … uses us to spread
the aroma of the knowledge of him everywhere.

—2 CORINTHIANS 2:14

We admire roses for their beauty, but before we get to enjoy a rose, it needs to be planted. What does it get planted in? Dirt. Then that rose has to push through a whole lot of dirt to get air. Do you ever feel like you're pushing through a whole lot of dirt just to get to air?

And then you start to bloom a little bit, and what happens? A gardener comes along and throws manure on you to help you grow more. Ever felt like you've had a little bit of that stuff thrown on you? Well, they say it's good for you.

A lot of times when we have to push through a lot of stuff, we'd rather run from it. But God promises that as we continue to push, the sunlight's coming. That's when you bloom in your full glory, and your fragrance fills the air.

What growing phase are you in? Buy a rose as a symbol of hope that Christ's aroma will spread through you today.

Walking Lessons

I will exalt you, LORD,
for you lifted me out of the depths.

—PSALM 30:1

When Trey and Austin were learning to walk, I was their cheerleader. Whether they were crawling, pulling themselves up on the table, or falling on their bottoms, I responded the same way. I smiled and clapped and exclaimed, "Good job!"

I wonder if they thought Mommy was foolish to make such a big deal about them lying there flat on their faces!

Many falls would follow before they mastered the art of walking and then running. But I never doubted them. I knew they would learn to walk eventually.

Wherever you are, wherever you have been, God has no doubts about your future. He believes in you, no matter how many times you have fallen so far. He has not reviewed your past and declared you unfit for service—though you may have declared yourself unfit. Unlike you, He is not focused on your falls. He is focused on your potential. He knows He can transform every fall from your past into a promising future.

In what ways have you fallen in the past? How did God come to your rescue and lift you "out of the depths"?

Don't Fear the Desert

"I will lead her into the wilderness
and speak tenderly to her."

—HOSEA 2:14

Are you familiar with Gomer? Not Gomer from Andy
Griffith's Mayberry (you know … "Shazaaaaaam!") but
Gomer from the Bible.

Gomer was the unfaithful wife of the prophet Hosea. In
Hosea 2, God described vividly how she chased after all the
wrong stuff and ended up powerless and poor. Yet in today's
verse we hear God promise to "speak tenderly to her."

Isn't that beautiful! Did you expect, as I did, for God to
say, "I will lead her into the desert and make her life even
more miserable"? Who expects the harsh desert to be a
place of tenderness? Yet the rest of Hosea 2 uses metaphor
to describe how Gomer's destroyed life will now be restored
by God.

Gomer's life led her into the wilderness, a harsh and
barren place. Yet she found God's tenderness there. Not judgment. Tenderness.

*What feels barren in your world? What losses do you mourn?
What behavior do you regret? This week, when you encounter
a desert moment, pause there. Don't fight it. Let God join you
in the desert and open your eyes to His tenderness.*

Think Small

> God chose the foolish things of the world
> to shame the wise; God chose the weak things
> of the world to shame the strong.
>
> —1 CORINTHIANS 1:27

David was the future king of Israel, yet he was the youngest boy in his family. When he faced his enemy, he boldly declared, "The LORD who rescued me from the paw of the lion and the paw of the bear will rescue me from the hand of this Philistine" (1 Samuel 17:37). Against a towering giant, a tiny pebble seemed insignificant. But David used what he had, and God toppled Goliath with it.

Another example: Compared to the riches many people enjoy, a widow's paltry offering might have been deemed unworthy. Yet this woman gave all that she had, and God has used her act to inspire people for generations. Jesus said of her, "This poor widow has put in more than all the others. All these people gave their gifts out of their wealth; but she out of her poverty put in all she had to live on" (Luke 21:3–4).

What "small" thing do you have that could make a difference in your world today? Your words for speaking encouragement? Your pen for writing an uplifting note? Your car for picking up a friend and taking her to lunch? Your silence for curbing an argument?

Our Prayer Helper

In the same way, the Spirit helps us in our weakness.
We do not know what we ought to pray for, but the Spirit
himself intercedes for us through wordless groans.

—ROMANS 8:26

A friend sent this quote to me: "If you only pray when you're in trouble, you're in trouble." Isn't that the truth! But while we might have more to pray about when we're in trouble, we don't always know how to put our anxiety or sadness or pain into words. That's where the Spirit comes in. He sees us struggling—sometimes literally moaning and groaning—and He translates that into words that go directly to God's heart.

What's nagging at you—about your life, a loved one? What are you having trouble putting into words? Give it to the Spirit and let him translate for you, then relax in the knowledge that God hears and understands.

Rubber Band Reminders

"Enlarge the place of your tent,
stretch your tent curtains wide, do not hold back."

—ISAIAH 54:2

I keep a box of rubber bands in my office. I look at them often and think of us. Yes, you and me. My rubber bands are all sizes, just like us; and they are all colors, just like us. And they all have to stretch to do what they were made to do. Again, just like us. We cannot reach our full potential until we are stretched. Stretched beyond our comprehension, our abilities, our past, our perspective—beyond our losses, frailty, and weaknesses—to be what God wants us to be and to do what He calls us to do.

Does that sound daunting? Try some baby steps. Wear a rubber band on your wrist today. Each time you have an opportunity to do something slightly (or very) uncomfortable, let that rubber band remind you that this is exactly how God plans to bring purpose and significance to your life. Then snap to it! If a little stretching is good for our bodily muscles, it must be good for our spiritual muscles as well.

Purpose from the Pain

Praise be to the God and Father of our Lord Jesus Christ,
the Father of compassion and the God of all comfort,
who comforts us in all our troubles, so that we can
comfort those in any trouble with the comfort
we ourselves receive from God.

—2 CORINTHIANS 1:3–4

In an online article for *Christianity Today*, Ann Voskamp tells the story of Nick Vujicic: "The morning of December 4, 1982, moments after his birth, they laid him in his mother's arms. She held a blunt torso. Her firstborn had no arms. No legs. No limbs." Voskamp continues, "I watch Nick … get himself a glass of water, type on his keyboard, share his story of hope with thousands of hurting people. God uses people willing to minister not out of their strengths but out of real weakness. Isn't that how God himself ministered to the world?"

God has a purpose for you and is using the pain of your past to lead you into that purpose. God sees something that you can't see: the story of His grace and comfort that you can take to other women living with the same burdens you live with.

Starting today, make this daily prayer a habit: "Lord, open my eyes to see the people You want me to encourage today." You'll be amazed by what happens next!

Trash Talk

The tongue is a small part of the body,
but it makes great boasts.
—JAMES 3:5

When Trey was a Little League pitcher, he came home distraught from one of his games, even though his team had won. "As I walk to the mound, I hear some of the ugliest comments," he said. "They call me a loser; they tell me I can't pitch. By the time I get out there, I could just cry. And Mom, these aren't kids talking that way. The adults are doing this."

After we talked a bit, I asked Trey if he had practiced throwing his curve balls. He had. Then I asked, "Do you go to every practice?"

"You know I do."

"Well then, Trey, here's the truth. Those voices can't take away your talent. They can't take away your hard work. The voices are only there to intimidate you. So from now on, when you start that walk from the dugout to the mound, think to yourself, *Hmm, they're really scared of me! They know what I'm about to do!* And rather than being intimidated, you're going be able to be the pitcher you've been called to be."

When you hear similar lies, say: "Wait a minute, that's not true. The truth is God's eyes have rested on me, and He is calling me to a task." Doesn't that give you a whole new perspective?

Words of Wonder

When your words came, I ate them;
they were my joy and my heart's delight.
—JEREMIAH 15:16

I used to think of the Bible as a book full of things we should not do—God's "stop that!" list. But over time, I have discovered that the Bible is God's personal letter to you and me, intended to draw us into a living relationship with Him by revealing how much He loves us and what wonders He has in store for us.

When I was little, my grandfather never had to say no to me. I loved him so much and wanted to please him so much that I watched him and learned what made him happy. That's what the Bible does for us when we open it with a childlike faith, believing it is God's love letter for us. As we get acquainted with the author, we don't need lists of what to do and not do. We see how much He loves us, and we are motivated by love to line up our lives with what pleases Him. That's a little girl with her father, right?

God, you don't say, "Read this book and get your act together." You say, "Come to me, My child. Sit in My lap and let Me tell you a story about how much I love you."

Is Anyone There?

When I called, you answered me;
you greatly emboldened me.

—PSALM 138:3

As you sip your morning coffee, you probably contemplate the decisions ahead of you for the day. I know I do. Some decisions are easily resolved. Figuring out what to wear or what's for dinner isn't going to matter beyond this day. But other decisions carry more weight: how to handle a current family crisis, what church to choose, where to tighten spending, what college is best for our kids, what God wants us to be doing in this season of our lives.

What questions are you seeking answers for today? Whatever lies unanswered before you, let me share a promise from the Bible that guarantees you don't have to go at your decision-making alone. It goes like this: "Call to me and I will answer you and tell you great and unsearchable things you do not know" (Jeremiah 33:3).

How comforting to know that God will not only hear our call to heaven today, but He will also answer. And what a confidence builder! Have a comforted, confident day.

When have you called out to God in the past week? How did He answer you?

When the Going Gets Tough

In humility value others above yourselves,
not looking to your own interests but each of you
to the interests of the others.

—PHILIPPIANS 2:3–4

Nothing in life is tougher than loving one another. If it were easy, we would all have happy families and thriving friendships! But the reality is, many times we give up on those relationships, turn our backs, throw up our hands, blame someone else, and walk away.

But God created us for relationship. He intends that the blessings of relationships far outweigh the burdens they create. That's why we must be stronger than our emotions, more humble than our pride, willing to see that others are as important as we are, determined and committed to staying and fighting for the relationship!

Some relationships may not seem humanly possible, but they are God possible. Pray for restored relationships today.

With Friends

A friend loves at all times,
and a brother is born for a time of adversity.
—PROVERBS 17:17

Seated in the back of the chapel, I wept as I watched women, from teens to senior citizens, struggle to their seats. Many slumped with exhaustion or rested on a neighbor's shoulder. Bald patches, sunken eyes, feeding tubes, wheelchairs—this is where life had brought them. And now God had brought me to Remuda Ranch, the world-renown treatment center for eating disorders. I knew the lies these women had believed about themselves, because I had believed them too.

We all fight lies—that we are not smart enough, funny enough, good enough, thin enough; that we are too marred by our sin to be usable, forgiven. We are tied to our past, fear blinds our future, and lies handcuff the possibilities of today. Not knowing what else to do, we smile and declare, "I'm fine."

Friendships can help break the bondage of lies you've been telling yourself, lies that keep you from living the fulfilled life Jesus died to give you. God has done His part. It's time to do yours—with friends!

What lies are you fighting? Instead of putting on a fake smile, instead of telling yourself everything's OK, reach out to someone today.

God Came Back

The angel of the LORD came back a second time.
—1 KINGS 19:7

If you read 1 Kings 19, you will meet Elijah, a faithful servant of God, who was worn out and, therefore, vulnerable. A verbal attack from the wicked Jezebel had sent weary Elijah running into the wilderness to get away from it all.

An angel from God brought Elijah food. About all Elijah could do in such a state of exhaustion was eat and sleep. But here's the part I love best: "The angel of the LORD came back a second time."

God never gives up on us. He understands us in all our weakness, and He will come back a second time, a third time, as many times as it takes to restore our bodies and spirits. So, if you are feeling that you have missed an opportunity from God, if you have been tuning out His whispers, or even if you are on the run from God this morning, it's OK. God knows where you are, and He will make Himself known to you again. He loves you enough to never, ever give up on you.

Thank you, Lord, for never giving up on me. And thank you for nourishing my spirit when the journey is too much for me.

Hearts and Hands

They realized that this work had been
done with the help of our God.
—NEHEMIAH 6:16

Have you noticed how easy it is to analyze, scrutinize, and pass judgment on what is going on around us? "What the world needs today is …"; "I cannot believe that group that calls itself Christian is …"; "If I were them I would …"

The truth is, if our world is going to become what God wants it to be, then we need people who will not just sit around and talk about how bad things are, but who will do something about it. Enter you and me! Sleeves rolled up and ready to serve.

God can use us just as He used Nehemiah's group of godly people. And those around us will realize our work is only accomplished because of God at work within us. I can think of no higher compliment than that God, the Lord of heaven, can be seen in the passion of our hearts and the work of our hands.

Set aside some time to read the book of Nehemiah, the story of a man who returns from exile to rebuild Jerusalem's walls. In what ways has God restored the broken-down walls in your life? What enemies have you faced along the way?

A Promising Outcome

"In this world you will have trouble. But take heart!
I have overcome the world."

—JOHN 16:33

Warning: Disappointments, hurts, trials, and even tribulations are coming your way.

Promise: That's not the end of your story.

Jesus doesn't paint a rosy picture in John 16:33, but He does proclaim a promising outcome. He quickly transforms bad news into good—and compels us to action. "I will have the final say about all your disappointments and hurts."

What hope this brings to any situation you may face today! God always has the final word about your life. He can turn to your good the hurt that is intended as evil against you; He can replace the shame and disgrace you bear with gain.

Imagine that you carry a huge tote filled with your fears, disappointments, and hurts. Now imagine yourself reaching into your heavy bag of troubles and handing each one to God. Take a deep breath of relief as you let each burden go. Then walk into your day knowing your cares and concerns are in good hands.

Wisdom from Above

The LORD gives wisdom; from his mouth
come knowledge and understanding.

—PROVERBS 2:6

A woman in our Bible study group had remained silent during our weeks of discussion and conversation. I knew she had valuable wisdom to share, so I wondered at her reticence. Finally, I questioned her privately and she admitted that someone she trusted had once made her feel incompetent. She had come to believe she had nothing worthwhile to share in a group like ours.

I immediately thought of Billy Graham's words: "Knowledge is horizontal; wisdom is vertical. It comes down from above." This woman had been convinced that because she was not "degreed up," she lacked wisdom. But her life experiences, viewed from the perspective of her deep vertical relationship with God, meant she was drawing upon the true Source of all wisdom.

Seek God in His Word today. Absorb His wisdom in its pages so you can share your life with confidence. And pray that God will speak wisdom, not foolishness, through you.

Confident Joy

"If you keep my commands, you will remain in my love. ...
I have told you this so that my joy may be in you
and your joy may be complete."

—JOHN 15:10–11

Complete joy—that's what Jesus promises to those who obey Him. And one reason for that joy is this: Once you step on the path He has shown you, He will walk it with you. This is not a God who asks the impossible of you and then waits for you to fail. No way! This is the God of whom Paul declared, "He who began a good work in you will carry it on to completion until the day of Christ Jesus" (Philippians 1:6).

In your quiet time today, reflect on the good work the Lord has begun in you. Write what you discover in your journal or describe your reflections to a friend. Last, give Him thanks for those blessings and for His faithfulness to you.

Unwelcome Visitors

Consider it pure joy ... whenever you face trials
of many kinds, because you know that the testing
of your faith produces perseverance.
Let perseverance finish its work so that you
may be mature and complete, not lacking anything.

—JAMES 1:2–4

Life is full of intruders. At the most inopportune time, they
burst into our lives to wreak havoc and chaos. No matter
how educated you are, how financially secure, how gifted, or
how spiritual, you cannot escape these intruders.

They go by many names: trials, conflicts, struggles, val-
leys, tests, loss, suffering.

My experience with life's intruders has taught me this:
It is not through perfect, trouble-free lives that Christ com-
pletes His work in us. Rather, it is through daily struggles,
disappointments, and even failures that Christ carries out the
unique plan He has designed for each of our lives.

*"Consider it pure joy" when I face all kinds of trials? I'm
having a hard time with that one, Lord. Your Word says that
the testing of my faith will eventually make me "mature and
complete." I'm just not feeling it yet! Give me the guidance
and strength to persevere in living out the unique plan you
designed for me. Amen.*

Looking Up

> "Truly I tell you, anyone who will not receive
> the kingdom of God like a little child will never enter it."
>
> —MARK 10:15

Children are always looking up. A child looks up at parents, teachers, even slightly older children. When we look up, we acknowledge that we don't know all the factors, we don't have all the answers, but we know someone who does. We look up to God for His perspective, because we know our perspective is limited at best.

The adult me is prone to say, "I can figure this out" or "I'll get control of this situation. I just need a little more time." But a child knows she can't figure it out because the answers and the circumstances are beyond her capacity or experience.

Lord, teach me to look up like a child, so I will enter your kingdom.

Taking Stock

Timothy has just now come to us from you and
has brought good news about your faith and love.

—1 THESSALONIANS 3:6

We women are always taking stock, aren't we! Sometimes we measure how far we've come—pounds lost, closets cleaned, promotions received. But most of the time, we focus on how far we have to go.

In her devotional *Battlefield of the Mind*, Joyce Meyer recalls, "I had times of great discouragement—as we all do. I remember times of bitter tears over my personal failures. But God kept nudging me forward. That's the secret of living the victorious Christian life—we move ahead little by little. It's an inching forward over months and years."

Instead of looking at how far we fall short, let's look at how far God has brought us. Let's celebrate the inches!

Today, take a few minutes to savor how far you have come. Are you worrying less? Are your words kinder? Are you less critical of your spouse and kids? Do you find humor where once you only felt irritation? Are you less stingy with your time, your praise, your smile? We don't often measure "progress" in these terms, but we should.

Pray This for Me

May the God of hope fill you with all joy and peace
as you trust in him, so that you may overflow with
hope by the power of the Holy Spirit.

—ROMANS 15:13

When I recently came across this verse in Romans, I thought, *I want to pray this for the people in my life.* Then I thought, *I hope someone prays this for me too!*

We begin every day with a new schedule, new responsibilities, new worries, new troubles (and some of the same old troubles too). But because our God is "the God of hope," we also begin each day with new hope. Let's help each other hang on to this great truth. Let's pray to be women who "overflow with hope."

Lord, thank you for filling me with peace and joy as I trust in you. Help me overflow with hope as well through the power of the Holy Spirit in me.

Freedom from Want

The LORD is my shepherd; I shall not want.
—PSALM 23:1 KJV

We have all walked through some hard times—even times we thought we'd never get through. Yet most of us can also look back and see that we have made it to the other side of those difficulties. Indeed, when I look back at God's faithful provision in the past it gives me great hope that He is still here for my current (and future) struggles.

Psalm 23 reminds us that God is alive and active in our lives. Consider the first few verses in The Message translation: "God, my shepherd! I don't need a thing. You have bedded me down in lush meadows, you find me quiet pools to drink from. True to your word, you let me catch my breath and send me in the right direction. Even when the way goes through Death Valley, I'm not afraid when you walk at my side. Your trusty shepherd's crook makes me feel secure" (vv. 1–4 MSG).

Take time today to read Psalm 23 in its entirety and note all the ways God has promised to set you free from want.

Smile at the Camera

The Lord delights in those who fear him,
who put their hope in his unfailing love.

—PSALM 147:11

Just about the time that school was letting out, a mom saw a storm warning on the news. She knew her daughter liked walking home from school, but because the rain was about to start, the mom jumped in her car and traced the path her daughter took. She was driving along, looking, looking, looking, and all of a sudden she saw her daughter in the distance.

The mom noticed that her daughter was doing something strange. She would take a couple of steps, the lightning would flash, and the daughter would stop and smile. Then the daughter would walk a few more steps, the lightning would flash again, and the daughter would look up and smile. Once the mom finally got her daughter safely in the car, she asked, "Honey, why were you stopping and smiling so much?" And the little girl said, "God kept taking my picture, so I just kept stopping and smiling at Him!"

I love that child's perspective—that God was enjoying her, approved of her, and showed His approval by snapping her photo.

Dear God, when I slide into believing you're not pleased with me, get my thinking back on track. Remind me of the little girl smiling at her admirer—you.

An Invitation to Decline

Do not be anxious about anything,
but in every situation, by prayer and petition,
with thanksgiving, present your requests to God.
—PHILIPPIANS 4:6

Wouldn't it be wonderful to wake up without a care in the world? But how often is that going to happen? We're tempted to worry before our feet even hit the floor. But there's hope. You see, temptations are merely invitations. We can choose to decline them.

Fear doesn't come from God. However, each time we're tempted to fear, God assures us of His faithfulness. So tucked within each impulse to worry today lies a personal invitation: Choose fear or walk in faith.

Philippians 4:6 acknowledges that worries and fears are part of life. But it also shows you aren't stuck in those fears; you've been empowered to choose a better way. You can choose to release each worry and fear to the power of prayer. And then you can be thankful. Your thanksgiving declares you believe that no matter your current circumstances, your God is actively working in your life—beyond what you can even imagine.

Fill your day with statements of release: "I release my fear of failure to you, Lord"; "I release my worries about the blood test to you, Lord." Decline the invitation to cling to your concerns. Choose instead the invitation of Philippians 4:6.

Thumbs Up for Time-Outs

"Come with me by yourselves
to a quiet place and get some rest."
—MARK 6:31

Go to time-out! For those of us who have raised or are now raising a child, these are our "go to" words. They allow clearer thinking and fresh perspective to invade a hypersensitive situation.

Have you ever wondered what an adult time-out might look like? What makes you breathe deeper and experience serenity and peace? Is it getting lost in a good book, walking through the park, getting a facial at the local spa? When the boys were little, my time-out was a fifteen-minute bubble bath at the end of the day. Now, when life gets crazy, I grab a cup of flavored coffee, curl up on the sofa, and flip through the pages of a favorite magazine.

It's not only OK to take a personal time-out; it's highly recommended. Everyone needs breaks from the drive to do, do, do. Be still, take a deep breath, relax. *Ahhhhh*. Nice, isn't it?

Where can you go today for a time-out and a small splurge?
You have permission to take it!

September

Bully-Proofing

"I am with you," declares the LORD.

—HAGGAI 1:13

School used to be a fairly safe place. But now we can't escape the news of widespread bullying.

As believers, we also have a bully (1 Peter 5:8). And he's not coming for our lunches; he's coming for our lives. He throws condescending remarks at us, reminds us of every mess-up, makes us feel small and insignificant ... need I go on?

When school kids are bullied, their parents can't always be there. But Jesus goes everywhere you go. He rides in the car with you, He sits in your meetings, He follows you into the ladies' room when your anxiety attack hits. So when your bully begins taunting you today, remind him who is by your side. At the mere whisper of Jesus' name, your bully must cease and desist.

Take some time to meditate on 1 Peter 5:8: "Be alert and of sober mind. Your enemy the devil prowls around like a roaring lion looking for someone to devour." How can you resist the wiles of the adversary today?

Dealing with Dirt

> Jesus knew ... that he had come from God
> and was returning to God; so ... he poured water
> into a basin and began to wash his disciples' feet.
>
> —JOHN 13:3–5

After dinner one evening, Jesus prepared to wash the disciples' feet. Peter reacted in horror at the thought. But Jesus insisted, and Peter relented.

In New Testament times, daily foot washing was essential. Open sandals plus dusty roads were a messy combination. Jesus' insistence on foot washing on this occasion, however, went deeper than hygiene. Jesus knew that daily cleansing was absolutely essential to our spiritual well-being. As long as we walk around in this world, we're going to get soiled by it. That soil leaves us feeling ashamed, guilty, longing to hide. But God doesn't see us that way. He says, "Here, let me take care of that."

We can respond in shame and sinful pride, like Peter did initially, and resist this astonishing offer from God. Or we can respond with grateful relief and surrender to the only cleansing routine that truly works.

In what areas of your life do you need God's cleansing touch? Ask Him to "wash your feet" today.

Heavenly Interruptions

And God said, "Let there be light."
—GENESIS 1:3

First this: God created the Heavens and Earth—all you see, all you don't see. Earth was a soup of nothingness, a bottomless emptiness, an inky blackness. God's Spirit brooded like a bird above the watery abyss.

God spoke: "Light!" And light appeared.

God saw that light was good and separated light from dark.

God named the light Day, he named the dark Night. (Genesis 1:1–5 MSG)

Darkness is a fact of life this side of heaven. Our hope, however, lies in this deep truth: God has been interrupting the darkness since the beginning of time. He will keep interrupting yours as well. Let this certainty give you renewed hope for what you're facing today.

In your quiet time today, reflect on ways that knowing God has brought more light into your life. Then thank Him.

Wearing Blinders

"We do not know what to do,
but our eyes are on you."

—2 CHRONICLES 20:12

Racehorses are easily distracted by what's beside them. That's where blinders come in. Blinders are leather flaps attached to a horse's bridle to prevent sideways vision. They keep a horse's focus solely on what lies ahead—the finish line.

What is distracting you today? Regret, worry, fear, doubt? Anger? A troubled relationship? Health challenges? A task bigger than your capacity? Try putting on your spiritual blinders. You may feel helpless and hopeless, but when you keep your eyes focused solely upon God, you find fresh energy to run the race, win the battle, seize the day, or any other analogy you want to use!

Focusing on God reveals that He has everything you need to meet your challenge. He is loving, powerful, merciful, strong, just, gracious, sovereign, and so much more. I think that's a good start, don't you?

Pray for someone today: "When _____ is facing a tough situation and doesn't know what to do, may her prayer be that of Jehoshaphat's: '[I] do not know what to do, but [my] eyes are on you.'"

Pick Me, Pick Me!

The eyes of the LORD search the whole earth in order to
strengthen those whose hearts are fully committed to him.
—2 CHRONICLES 16:9 NLT

Do you remember when you were in elementary school,
and the PE teacher would select a team captain, and
then the captain would have to choose the team? Were you
one of the first ones selected or, like me, were you near the
end? Ugh! I remember the silent pleading within me: *Pick
me, pick me!*

Someone is still picking team members today. God is
actively looking to add to His team—that's amazing! And isn't
it inspiring to imagine Him searching our homes, churches,
communities, cities, and beyond and asking, "Whom shall
I send into this school or to the football games … into this
department store … into this neighborhood to live in this
for-sale house?"

Maybe you're thinking, *Sure it would be amazing, but I
would never be picked.* But you're wrong. God doesn't need
your strength, your talents, or your plans. He simply wants
your willing, obedient heart. We can say, "Pick me, pick
me," knowing He *will* pick us. And more than that, He will
empower and equip us to accomplish His will.

*Lord, send me, so that all the world can see you have a place
for them on your team as well.*

Stable in the Storm

We will no longer be ... tossed back and forth.
—EPHESIANS 4:14

Did you watch the coverage of Hurricane Sandy several years ago?

As news teams descended on the mid-Atlantic coast, I particularly noticed the cameramen. Even though they had their heavy equipment to anchor them, these men and women struggled to stand steady against the force of the storm.

In contrast were the shore birds. These tiny creatures—weighing mere ounces—danced in the sand. Gusting winds didn't toss them about, and torrential rains didn't distract them.

Imagine if you were one of those dancing birds—no longer tossed about by the storms of life. God's Word says you can be!

SEPTEMBER 7

Fight and Feed

Fight the good fight of the faith.
—1 TIMOTHY 6:12

Doubt will inevitably enter your mind, but it doesn't need to affect your actions. Fight for your faith by fighting against doubt. And how do you fight against doubt? By feeding your faith. One way to feed your faith is to replace your "stinking thinking" with God's thinking. For centuries, people have done this by memorizing truth from God's Word. It's not hard!

We aren't stuck with doubt. We can break free from it by filling our minds with truth. The truth will set us free.

Pick one verse this week that encourages you. Write it on index cards or stickies that you place around the house or in your car. Or enter it in your smartphone or on your tablet, and have the device "ding" hourly to remind you to read your verse. By the end of the week, I bet you'll know it by heart, and the stinking thinking will be history.

Mission Possible

"With man this is impossible,
but with God all things are possible."
—MATTHEW 19:26

What is God asking you to do today? What have you been putting off? I know what it's like to keep saying, "One day, God, one day." But could one day be this day?

Ask God what He wants to tell you about His next step for you—the step beyond what you know is possible, beyond what you know you can pull off on your own. Where does He want to take you that is beyond your strength, talents, willpower, and abilities? What passion has He put on your heart that you really want to pursue but are afraid is not possible?

Read Matthew 19:26, imagining Jesus saying those words directly to you. How does that change your perspective on the adventure ahead of you?

Picture This

> "I am the vine; you are the branches.
> If you remain in me and I in you, you will bear much fruit;
> apart from me you can do nothing."
>
> —JOHN 15:5

A kindergarten teacher was walking around her classroom while her students drew pictures. One student was scribbling so intently that the teacher asked what she was drawing. The little girl replied, "I'm drawing a picture of my friend, Jesus." The teacher said, "Oh honey, nobody really knows for sure what Jesus looked like." The little girl, without missing a beat, responded, "They will in a minute."

Our lives are constantly drawing a picture of Jesus for those around us. The more we remain in Him, soaking up His presence, the more accurate that picture will be. I'm not saying that the more perfect a picture of *you* that you draw, the more people will recognize Jesus. It isn't about your perfection. It's about Jesus being visible in the *imperfect* you.

When we skip spending time in Jesus' presence and focus entirely on serving Him, what comes out of us is a whole lot of us—and very little of Jesus.

I don't want people to see a whole lot of me today; I want them to see a whole lot of you, Jesus. I want them to know who I've been spending time with!

Puzzling Plans

"You meant evil against me, but God meant it for good
in order to bring about this present result."

—GENESIS 50:20 NASB

Joseph was one of the good guys. So where in the world was God during those dark nights in the pit, or when Joseph was being falsely accused? Only when you get to the end of Joseph's story can you say, "Wow, God really did have a plan." Good thing Joseph never gave up, right?

We never really know what God is up to, but we know He promises that all things are working for the good of those who love Him (Romans 8:28). And we know He promises never to leave us as these plans slowly unfold. Whatever your current struggle, one day you will be exactly where you need to be. And it will be good.

What will you choose to believe about God's plan today, even if you can't see a hopeful ending?

Am I the Only One?

Your enemy the devil prowls around ... looking for
someone to devour. Resist him, standing firm in the faith,
because you know that the family of believers throughout
the world is undergoing the same kind of sufferings.

—1 PETER 5:8–9

Misery loves company, and while I wish no misery on
anyone, that old saying comes to my mind each time
I read the above verse. Oddly, it makes me feel a bit better.

Have you ever thought, *Am I the only one?* Everyone at
the mall or in the office looks so together and worry-free. No
one else seems to be struggling. This verse says otherwise:
Everyone around you today—and around the world—is fighting some type of battle. Take comfort in knowing you are not
alone. When God drew you to Himself, He drew you into a
family. You can resist and stand firm alongside the rest of your
family of faith.

*Consider these men: Moses had a staff, David a simple
slingshot, and Samson a jawbone. And these women: A
widow had a couple of coins, Rahab a string, and Dorcas a
needle. What is something you can use to resist the enemy
today?*

Regret and Revelation

> "Here is a boy with five small barley loaves and
> two small fish, but how far will they go among so many?"
> —JOHN 6:9

The boy in John 6 captures my imagination. I wonder if, before he left home, the boy said, "Mom, do I really have to take this sack lunch? Can't I go to the concession stands and buy the good food like everyone else?"

And when his lunch became the center of attention, did he feel embarrassed? Did he think, *Now everyone knows we're poor?* I bet his lunch bag had been eating at his confidence all day, making him feel inferior to the people around him.

Then, the first miracle of the day occurred. No, not the changing of a meager lunch into a feast, but the changing of "if only" into "what if." The transformation from "If only I had more to offer" to "What if I just give Jesus all that I have?"

The truth is, the boy had all he needed—a heart for Jesus and his little brown bag. And we know that in the end, he handed it all over to Jesus, and Jesus did what no one else could do: He took what the boy had to offer and multiplied its blessings.

How can you bless someone today with what's inside your "little brown bag"?

Perfect Math

How abundant are the good things that you have stored up
for those who fear you, ... on those who take refuge in you.

—PSALM 31:19

God has called you to so much more than a life of hiding
and self-protection. He wants to take all you have always deemed worthless and insignificant, those things that
have been eating away at your heart, because He intends to
use them to feed hope to the famished multitudes you walk
among each day. God's perfect love plus your imperfect life
add up to abundant blessing.

*When you think of abundance, what images come to
mind? How might your life—mundane as it may seem to
you—change if you viewed it from this new perspective of
abundance? That's how God views it.*

Only Christ

See to it that no one takes you captive through hollow
and deceptive philosophy, which depends on human
tradition and elemental spiritual forces of this world
rather than on Christ.

—COLOSSIANS 2:8

Finding God's timing and plan for healing the burdens you carry will come only through your relationship with Jesus. You can consult all the experts of the day. You can read the self-help books and magazines. But Paul, the gifted philosopher of the Bible, knew those efforts would lead nowhere. He is not condemning philosophy and other pursuits in the above verse; he simply understands that the world's timing, solutions, and ideologies do not have the power to heal our broken hearts and broken lives. Only Christ does. And Christ works through relationship.

Is it hard for you to get your mind around what a relationship with God would look like? Take some time today to think about what makes any close relationship work: spending time together, talking a lot about everything under the sun, and really listening. Pick one of those qualities and identify one way you can do that with God. It's so much better than buying another self-help book!

Memories of Encouragement

I constantly remember you in my prayers.
Recalling your tears, I long to see you, so that I may be
filled with joy. I am reminded of your sincere faith.

—2 TIMOTHY 1:3–5

The apostle Paul and Timothy had been through a lot together: wonderful, celebratory times and dark, agonizing times. Their faith in God and belief in each other had allowed them to survive and bonded them in such a way that, even when they were separated, their memories brought joy, strength, and encouragement.

John Maxwell says, "Believing in people before they have succeeded is the key to motivating them to reach their fullest potential." According to Paul, Timothy's sincere faith was passed down to him by his grandmother, Lois, and his mother, Eunice. They believed in his potential as a man of God and invested in him accordingly.

Who has believed in you and motivated you toward your Christ-given potential? Spend some time thanking God for each person. Before this day ends, send one of those people an e-mail or note to thank her for the role she has played in your life.

Free Failing

"The LORD does not look at the things people look at.
People look at the outward appearance,
but the LORD looks at the heart."

—1 SAMUEL 16:7

For years, I was imprisoned in the performance trap. Sing in the choir? Oh no, I might sing off key. Join a Bible study? Oh no, I might have trouble finding Genesis. Talk to my new neighbor? What if I get tongue-tied?

I have since learned a freeing secret about our great God: He's not looking for perfect performance; He's looking for humble hearts. He beams with pride when I step outside my comfort zone to welcome a new neighbor. He doesn't notice if I jumble up my words (my neighbor probably doesn't notice either). I think He preens a little, on my behalf, when He peers into my heart and sees my only motive was to go beyond the confinements of self into the freedom of serving Him.

Ask your Father today to free you from an obsession with perfect performance. Ask Him for an adventurous heart that isn't afraid to fail. After all, because of Him, no failure is ever final.

How to Talk to Yourself

"When [the devil] lies, he speaks his native language,
for he is a liar and the father of lies."

—JOHN 8:44

God says you are good—very good. He says you are worthy, significant, and born with a purpose and a plan. He says you are lovable, likable, and equipped with all good things. He says you are an overcomer (1 John 2:13; 4:4), a success story, and filled with His power. God says you are the apple of His eye (Zechariah 2:8). He delights in you (Zephaniah 3:17), and He has chosen you to be His beloved child (Romans 8:15).

Do you realize that when you speak in a derogatory way about yourself, you're disagreeing with what God says about you and agreeing with the enemy?

When is the last time you told yourself you are God's beloved child? Today, speak truth to yourself! Speak life into dry bones (Ezekiel 37:1–14)! Agree with God.

Sink or Swim

Peter got down out of the boat, walked on the water and
came toward Jesus. But when he saw the wind, he was
afraid and, beginning to sink, cried out, "Lord, save me!"
Immediately Jesus reached out his hand and caught him.

—MATTHEW 14:29–31

Here we see Peter moving from an earnest desire to demonstrate his faith to a frightened floundering. When Peter lost sight of the one he wanted to please, he began to sink.

I too was about to sink in my own sea of doubt when God reached out to me with this story and showed me what to do. First, I had to get out of the boat, the place I had found comfortable and safe from the storms of life. The place where I could hide and pretend. Second, I had to go alone. Peter didn't wait to see if all his buddies were coming and neither could I. Was I willing to be the first one to take off my masks? Maybe even the only one? Third, I needed to keep my eyes on Jesus.

Now that He has shown me a different way of life, I have to stay focused on following only Him—no matter how stormy it gets outside the boat.

What is God saying to you through this story? (See Matthew 14:22–33.)

Approach with Confidence

In him and through faith in him we may approach
God with freedom and confidence.

—EPHESIANS 3:12

A little boy found himself in big trouble. He finally gave up trying to explain himself and find forgiveness with his mom. As he trudged up the stairs to his room, his mom asked, "Where are you going?" He responded, "I'm headed up to talk to Jesus. I think I have a better chance of Him forgiving me than you."

What a great truth in which to find your freedom today! We will mess up in life—intentionally and unintentionally. At those times when we most feel like running away from God, we can run toward Him. Jesus did that for us. He's the reason we can approach God with freedom and confidence.

What, if anything, stops you from running into Jesus' arms when you need Him the most?

First Focus

I am afraid that just as Eve was deceived by
the serpent's cunning, your minds may somehow be
led astray from your sincere and pure devotion to Christ.

—2 CORINTHIANS 11:3

Paul wrote these words to the Corinthian believers because false teaching was undermining their devotion. What threatens your devotion today? Sometimes the threat is as subtle as a shift in focus. You can be so focused on getting the laundry folded, making one more phone call, or baking one more batch of cookies for the kids' lunches that you forget to spend any time with God, focusing on Him.

No matter what else is on your to-do list, commit to spending ten minutes with God today—and tomorrow, and so on. You'll be surprised by how thirsty your heart is for His company. And, I believe, you'll be surprised at how quickly your focus returns to the things that matter most.

Did you try this? Did you set aside ten minutes for God today? How do you think it affected the focus of your day?

Never Forsaken

"Be strong and courageous. … Do not be afraid
or discouraged, for the LORD God, my God, is with you.
He will not fail you or forsake you."

—1 CHRONICLES 28:20

Belief in God's greater plan for me has allowed me to look at all situations differently. I've been encouraged even in my sorrow by the knowledge that God is working in and through me. Belief that God has a plan for me has opened my eyes to see unexpected blessings tucked in among some of my painful or unexplainable situations.

Perhaps the wounds of one friend will open our eyes to the nurturing heart of another friend. Maybe the pain of watching a child struggle in school will reveal the determination and persistence that is part of that child's God-given character. A painful season in a marriage may prepare a couple to minister more compassionately to other couples. What I know for sure is that because God is present in the trial—and you can be sure He is—there are treasures to pluck from the darkness.

That's why King David could state with such confidence, "Be strong and courageous."

Where do you need courage today? Watch that courage
emerge as you thank God for His promise to be with you
in every challenge. He will never fail you or forsake you.
Breathe in those great truths and then get to work!

You Are Here

> "Here is my servant, whom I uphold,
> my chosen one in whom I delight."
>
> —ISAIAH 42:1

*Y*ou Are Here.

These three words on the mall directory relieved my fatigue and frustration. I knew my destination, but I also had to know where I *was* to get to where I wanted to be.

There's something even more important, however, than knowing where you are; it's knowing who you are. In today's verse, Isaiah refers to Jesus, the Chosen One, but you've been chosen too. And when God chooses you He also loves you and delights in you. You never leave His mind or escape His sight. He knows and understands you better than you know yourself—even your failings and struggles. And yet His resolve remains the same: He loves you. He delights in you. You can do nothing to make Him love you more, and you can do nothing to cause Him to love you less.

Put another way: The good news is not that you love God; it is that He loves you! Not that you have found God (though that is good), but that in Him you have been found. As the directory says, *You Are Here.* Called by Him, chosen by Him, upheld by Him, the one in whom He delights.

How has life left you feeling lost and fatigued? When this happens, knowing who you are—instead of where you are—will take you where you need to be.

The Size of Spectacular

"Who dares despise the day of small things?"
—ZECHARIAH 4:10

A friend and I were talking recently about our deep desire to be used by God. We admitted that our strong "want to" didn't guarantee an "easy do." Assorted obstacles can get in our way, including what we think "being used by God" really means.

Two mistaken beliefs can prevent us from responding to God's call. The first is the belief that mission fields must be far flung, like Somalia or Bangladesh. The second is the belief that our service must be dramatic and spectacular. Have you ever felt "underwhelmed" by what God is asking of you? Your block might not seem like much of a mission field, and sharing your garden tomatoes with your neighbor may lack dramatic flair. But when we recognize that God longs to use us right where He has placed us, we will joyfully grab opportunities at the grocery store, in our neighborhoods, at the gym, and, yes, even in our places of worship.

Open your eyes today to those in your small world who need kindness, encouragement, help, and generosity. What can you do to reach out? Even though your actions may seem ordinary to you, they become pretty spectacular to the recipient.

A World of Wonders

Many, LORD my God, are the wonders you have done,
the things you planned for us.

—PSALM 40:5

When students were asked to list the Seven Wonders of the World, a teacher noted that one student hadn't turned in her paper, then asked if the girl was confused by the assignment.

"Yes, a little," the girl answered. "I couldn't quite make up my mind because there are so many."

The teacher suggested that she read aloud what she had on her list so far.

The girl hesitated, then read, "I think the Seven Wonders of the World are: to see, to taste, to touch, to hear, to feel, to laugh or smile, and most of all, to love."

Doesn't that story take your breath away!

I hope you will walk through this day with wide-eyed wonder at the treasures in your life that you can see, taste, touch, hear, feel, laugh at, and love. With each wonder you notice, whisper (or shout!) "Thank You!" to God, who made all wonders.

Wherever, Whenever, Whomever

> "Whatever you did for one of the least of these
> brothers and sisters of mine, you did for me."
> —MATTHEW 25:40

There's no formula for how God will use you to bless others. He doesn't make any two people exactly alike, and I suspect He doesn't have any identical plans for His people. He is ever creating. Our job is to notice what He is creating and where and with whom. That's called discernment.

The grumpy cashier, the teacher who yells at your child, the person conducting your job interview, the nurse administering your chemotherapy—hidden among these people are numerous opportunities to join God in His ministry of healing and hope. When you embrace this unseen reality, you will no longer sit in a corner, stuck, wondering when God will use you. Instead, you'll be set free to spread blessings wherever you go—and to set *others* free.

Show me, Lord, how to find the "the least of these" among us.
What would you have me do for them?

Poor Me

> "Blessed are the poor in spirit,
> for theirs is the kingdom of heaven."
> —MATTHEW 5:3

Being poor in spirit is not about always being down in the mouth. "Poor, pitiful me!" It's not about being on the verge of financial bankruptcy. Rather, to be poor in spirit is to recognize we are *spiritually* bankrupt before God. To be poor in spirit is to have a humble opinion of ourselves, to realize our very existence is by God's gift and grace.

Being poor in spirit gives birth in us to a deep longing to stay connected with God wherever He places us, to bear what He lays upon us, to go where He leads us. We empty ourselves of our self. No pride. No self-reliance. We know our next breath depends on God and not any power we possess.

The poor in spirit know it's not about their gifts or talents, their looks or wardrobe, their wealth or status. It's all about God. It's only about God. To grasp that and to live by it is to discover that the entire kingdom of heaven is ours.

Take a look at the Beatitudes today (Matthew 5:1–12).
Besides "the poor in spirit," who else is blessed in God's eyes?
Which of those surprises you the most?

Facing Fear

God has not given us the spirit of fear,
but of power and of love and of a sound mind.

—2 TIMOTHY 1:7

You don't need to be ashamed of your fears; we all have them. But you also don't need to let your fears cripple you.

Jesus said to a blind man and a bleeding woman, "Your faith has healed you" (Mark 10:52, 5:34). He says the same to us today. Faith trumps fear. Whatever you face today, don't let fear overtake you. Cast off the identify you've given yourself of "fearful woman" and take on your new identity of "woman of faith." Then take a step of faith, past the boundary of your fear, into a new possibility!

What do you fear today? Loneliness? Rejection? Failure to measure up? You could probably create a list of fears a mile long, couldn't you? For now, focus on one of those fears. What baby step can you take toward being a woman of faith, not fear?

Wisdom from a GPS

I will instruct you and teach you in the way you should go;
I will counsel you with my loving eye on you.

—PSALM 32:8

Where are you ... really?

The GPS in our car inspired that question. You see, to get to my desired destination, I have to put the destination's address into the system, then I must enter my starting point. But suppose I'm dreading the length of the trip and want to make it seem shorter. Well, I could put in a starting address that's at the midpoint of the trip instead of at the beginning. That would cut down on the distance, right? But it would be foolish. It would have nothing to do with reality. The GPS can only help me if I face the truth about my starting point.

How many of us never get to where we want to go because we are not willing to admit where we really are? We have a clear destination: to become all God has created us to be and to fulfill our unique plan. But we fail to recognize the way to do that—namely, by being honest with God, ourselves, and others about where we currently are.

Forget how long the trip may take. Tell the truth about your starting point, then prepare to enjoy the journey to your destination.

Superwoman Syndrome

May I never boast except
in the cross of our Lord Jesus Christ.

—GALATIANS 6:14

God created us and declared us "very good" (Genesis 1:31). But how hard is it for us to think of ourselves as very good? Most of us find it easier to think, *If only I could be more, do more, have more …*

I call this the Superwoman Syndrome—the constant striving and questing to do it all and do it all perfectly. We all feel driven to put on our superhero capes and conquer the world.

But what if having more power is really about *surrendering* more power? John the Baptist put it this way: "He must become greater; I must become less" (John 3:30).

You see, as powerful as we are—and we are a talented, successful bunch—who can write a check large enough to ease the pain of losing a loved one? Who has the power to remove the shame of losing a job? Who can fill the void of an empty nest?

We can't. But here's the power we *do* have: We can quietly slip into each of those situations and share the only true source of power—Jesus Christ.

Instead of showing off your superwoman cape, how you can point people to the cross (the only power that truly leads to the abundant life)?

Transformed Junk

If I must boast,
I will boast of the things that show my weakness.
—2 CORINTHIANS 11:30

Have you ever thought, *My life is nothing to brag about?* Great! You're exactly the kind of person God is looking for.

We mistakenly think God can use only the good stuff in our lives. Because we do not have a flawless past, we are convinced we have nothing to offer Him. We lose hope.

God can and does use our successes, talents, and gifts, but He also uses our hurts and burdens for His good purposes. In fact, it's most often our pain that people can relate to, and where they find hope. Right now, offer the junk in your life to God—the flaws, mistakes, sin, foolishness, weaknesses. He can transform them in ways you cannot imagine.

Father, you turn things upside down! It makes sense that you would use my talents and abilities—you gave them to me. Now you are telling me that you want to use the messes in my life. I can't quite wrap my head around that, but I thank you for loving all of me, even the junky parts.

October

Freed from Busyness

"Walk with me and work with me. ...
Learn the unforced rhythms of grace."
—MATTHEW 11:29–30 MSG

There's a saying, "If the devil can't make you bad, he'll make you busy!" Being busy makes us feel important. It distracts us from the pain we carry in our hearts. Our "availability" and energy impress people. But busyness also enslaves us. It prevents us from embracing opportunities God brings our way.

Our ridiculous to-do lists reflect the tendency of some of us to embrace *every* opportunity. But I'd like to focus on a particular kind of opportunity—the kind God has custom-designed for you. The kind that takes into account your pain, failures, missteps, and burdens and transforms them into blessings. Those are the opportunities worth embracing! Are you free to embrace them, or are you in bondage to too many other demands for your time and energy?

God's custom-made opportunity for you may be right around the corner. What do you need to get off your to-do list, so you're free to be a blessing?

A Parent You Can Trust

Consider it pure joy … whenever you face trials
of many kinds, because you know that the testing
of your faith produces perseverance … so that you
may be mature and complete, not lacking anything.

—JAMES 1:2–4

When my boys were small, they dreaded their inocula-
tions. So did I. How could I explain that the nurse was
inflicting pain on them *with my permission*? What did they
understand about big concepts like "future health and safety"? I'll never forget the accusation in those big, sad eyes.

Similarly, your heavenly Parent feels no pleasure in your
pain. Yet He knows, as I knew with my boys, that the pain is
not wasted. He is seeing to your spiritual health and well-being. Find hope today in knowing that, though you may not
understand Him, you can trust Him.

*Have you ever undergone a medical procedure that was
painful at the time but resulted in better health afterwards?
What parallels do you see between that experience and a
difficult situation you are in currently?*

Living beyond Your Means

Now to him who is able to do immeasurably more
than all we ask or imagine,
according to his power that is at work within us.

—EPHESIANS 3:20

What would it look like for you to live beyond your means—not financially but spiritually?

All through the Bible, people were asked to do what was beyond their capacity or comfort or natural ability so that others would be reached with God's love and generosity. How would the Hebrews have crossed the Red Sea had Moses not stood up to Pharaoh, demanding freedom for God's people (Exodus 5–15)? How would the Israelites have won the battle for Jericho had Rahab been unwilling to welcome the two spies into her home (Joshua 2)? What would have happened to the five thousand had there not been one little boy who was willing to sacrifice his lunch (Matthew 14)?

Seek to do what you know you cannot do, or what you don't want to do.

Today, say yes to what you know you cannot do without God! God is ready to do "immeasurably more" than you can imagine in your life. What will your miracle be?

Say What?

I was shown mercy so that in me, the worst of sinners,
Christ Jesus might display his immense patience … for
those who would believe in him and receive eternal life.

—1 TIMOTHY 1:16

"I never quite understood why Jesus chose the individuals he did," writes Jarrid Wilson, author of *Jesus Swagger*. "He didn't call the popular, rich, or successful to further his ministry, but rather, the poor, broken, and faithful. I can only imagine how confused the Pharisees and religious leaders must have been while looking at the team of people the proclaimed Savior had gathered together."

When I sensed God urging me to start sharing about what He's done in my own life, I assumed He wanted me to talk about how good and perfect my life was now. I was wrong. "No, Kim," He said, "I want you to share the messy things I have gotten you through. By doing so, you are not only glorifying me, but you are also connecting to people." Ever since, I've talked about God's grace. That's what people need to hear: that no matter what they're struggling with, He will forgive them and help them out of the pit they're in.

Can you recall a time when your struggles helped you connect with another person more effectively than your triumphs would have?

Small Matters

Come, my children, listen to me;
I will teach you the fear of the LORD.

—PSALM 34:11

A few years ago a neighbor, and mother of six little ones, sent me a school assignment her oldest had completed. It was a list of questions little Madison had answered. One question asked, "Who do you trust?" Written in Madison's familiar penmanship was her answer: *Ms. Kim.* The next question asked, "How has this person helped you?" Madison wrote, *She sits and talks to me.*

Madison's parents love her and her siblings in the best way. Yet God clearly also has a role for me to play with Madison. As I reflected on this I was drawn back to when I was a little girl. At a crucial period, a woman took time for me. She sat with me and talked about whatever I chose. She shared with me the story of Jesus, and she showed me the love of Jesus.

I am thankful God prompted me, even if I was unaware of His prompting, to slow down, sit still, talk, and listen to this little one as she dances through my life.

What small person do you know who would benefit from a small pause in your hectic schedule, a small word of affirmation, or a small gesture of caring?

In Whose Steps?

I will study your teachings and follow your footsteps.
—PSALM 119:15 CEV

How many times has an usher or waiter said to you, "If you will just follow me"? And what did you do? You followed after him, confident that your guide would get you to your desired destination. We, as believers, are also guides of a sort, showing others the way to God's hope, love, and healing.

The thought of others following in our footsteps may seem daunting until we remember Abraham, Moses, and David. They were great leaders, and multitudes followed them. But they were also flawed. Their worthiness was not rooted in how perfect they were, but in the God they followed. We need not put ourselves under pressure to perform perfectly. What matters is that we let people know whom we follow.

Today, Lord, help me to "meditate on your precepts and consider your ways" (Psalm 119:15).

Let It Shine

Then you will shine among them like stars in the sky.
—PHILIPPIANS 2:15

How are we believers supposed to stand out in this world? We all know it's not by being perfect because, really, who is? We know it's not by crazy predictions—I suppose some believers stand out with their end-times warnings, but in a very awkward way. Being judgmental "Bible thumpers" or saying thee, thy, and thou won't impress anyone either. So, when the Scriptures declare that people will recognize us as followers of Christ, exactly what does that mean?

In the verse above, the apostle Paul likens believers to stars. I love that!

God created stars to shine. That is their purpose—and ours. As God's creations, we will be invited into situations where we can make a difference. What kinds of situations? Perhaps a gossipy session with the girls, or an encounter with a rude bystander at the bank, or a conversation with an obnoxious supervisor—dark, hurtful, potentially explosive situations where something as simple as a gentle word, a kind response, or an understanding smile turns on a light in the darkness.

Today, take a closer look at those dark situations in which you find yourself and ask, "God, is this my time to shine?"

Declaration of Hope

> I consider that our present sufferings are not worth
> comparing with the glory that will be revealed in us.
> —ROMANS 8:18

I will never forget watching the news about South Carolina First Lady Jenny Sanford's divorce-driven departure from the governor's mansion. As she exited the mansion into a sea of reporters, I marveled at her courage in the face of relentless questions.

Jenny acknowledged her devastation. She conceded the path before her was not clear and would be walked one day—and one gut-wrenching decision—at a time. But amid her pain Jenny proclaimed confidence that her path would lead to rebuilding and healing and that she and her boys would "not only survive but would thrive."

As believers we are called not only to survive devastation in our lives but to be better because of it. That's when the world sees much more than a group of good little people; the world sees a God who is bigger than anything we might have to handle.

What pain have you lived through, what burdens do you still carry? What might happen if you allow God to use your secret pain to bring hope to others who hurt? Ask God to lead you to someone today who needs to hear you proclaim the kind of hope Jenny Sanford declared.

Dew Drops

"Be still, and know that I am God."
—PSALM 46:10

I t is early morning. For some reason my body thinks it doesn't need sleep. As I sit at my computer, I can see most of the homes in my neighborhood. All is silent and still. There are no lights on. All little and big bodies are being rested and renewed in the stillness of this night.

Another form of refreshing comes only in the night: the dew. Dew is God's way of refreshing and renewing the earth's vegetation, but dew only comes during rest and stillness.

Are you feeling exhausted? Have you got the *blahs*, a sense of the same-old-same-old? Perhaps you need some heavenly dew. God invites us to be still. Stillness isn't easy for many of us. But after just a few minutes of stillness with God, we can be transformed from feeling *blah* to blessed. I'm pretty sure I can make time for that. How about you?

I invite you to start taking just a few moments each day to quiet yourself, open up God's Word, pray, and enjoy time with Him.

Misery Requires Company

Turn to me and be gracious to me,
for I am lonely and afflicted.

—PSALM 25:16

Even the most spiritual person can be overwhelmed. Take Martha, for example, busy with the Lord's work, who felt she was the only one trying to please Jesus. Her loneliness fed a judgmental spirit and caused a verbal assault on her sister (Luke 10:38–40).

And then there was Elijah (1 Kings 17–19). This great prophet raised the widow's son and defeated the prophets of Baal at Carmel. A spiritual giant, wouldn't you say? Yet he ran away like a scaredy-cat after a woman named Jezebel threatened him. He fled into the wilderness, plopped down under a broom tree, and, overcome by depression, prayed, "Take my life; I am no better than my ancestors" (19:4).

We'll all have moments like Martha's and Elijah's. We're going to get stuck or all wadded up because of something that was said or done. We can, though, choose a different path—the path to a good friend.

Think about it. Would you rather spend the day wallowing under a broom tree? Or would you rather spend it with _____? *Fill in the blank and make the phone call. I bet you'll discover that two are better than one.*

Who Do You Think You Are?

In Christ you have been brought to fullness.

—COLOSSIANS 2:10

I recently overheard a frustrated mom ask her disobedient daughter, "Who do you think you are, young lady?" As a parent with two grown sons, I can relate. I have been there, done that.

I can relate on a spiritual level as well. I hear that same question in my head: *Who do you think you are?* Interestingly, I don't hear those words when I am disobedient, but when I am striving to live obediently. And it's not a parental voice—my heavenly Father's—speaking those words, but rather the voice of my enemy.

When you hear "Who do you think you are?" you can respond with who you *know* you are:

- I am God's daughter (John 1:12).
- I am God's workmanship (Ephesians 2:10).
- I have a great purpose (Jeremiah 29:11).
- I am forgiven (Romans 8:1–2).
- I can do all things through Christ (Philippians 4:13).

This is *God's solid truth* about us.

When you start your day, think on the affirmations above— even better, think on them moment by moment, all day long. That way you'll be ready the next time a snide little voice whispers, "Who do you think you are?"

Giants in the Land

Let no man's heart fail because of ... this Philistine.
—I SAMUEL 17:32 KJV

In *Facing the Giants*, high school football coach Grant Taylor (played by Alex Kendrick) prays, "Lord Jesus, would you help me? I need you. Lord, I feel that there are giants of fear and failure staring down at me, waiting to crush me. And I don't know how to beat 'em, Lord. I'm tired of being afraid. Lord, if you want me to do something else, show me. If you don't want me to have children, so be it. But you're my God. You're on the throne. You can have my hopes and my dreams. Lord, give me something. Show me something."

What giant do you fear today? What might you be giving up by not confronting your giant? God had appointed David to be king twenty years before he actually wore the crown. Twenty years! Yet the obstacles David confronted during those two decades—including bears, lions, and the giant Goliath—gave him confidence and courage to fulfill his ultimate God-called role as King of Israel.

Today, do as David (and Coach Taylor) did. First acknowledge your personal giants—those things that intimidate, overwhelm, or defeat you. Then, rather than running from them, stop and face your giants. You'll be one step closer to whatever great appointment God has already made for you.

Truth to Live By

Whatever is true, whatever is noble,
whatever is right, whatever is pure, whatever is lovely,
whatever is admirable—if anything is excellent
or praiseworthy—think about such things.

—PHILIPPIANS 4:8

When events appear to defy what you know to be true about God and His posture toward you, the verse above can be a starting place for reminding you to look for the right kind of truth to live by:

1. Is it true?
2. Is it noble?
3. Is it right?
4. Is it pure?
5. Is it lovely?
6. Is it admirable?
7. Is it excellent?
8. Is it praiseworthy?

Remember, it is not what is actually occurring in our lives that affects our behavior but rather what we believe about what is occurring.

Ask God to help you see your circumstances through His eyes.

If you're not sure of the meaning of some of the words in the above list, try reading Philippians 4:8 in a few other translations. A small tweak of a word can enrich our understanding.

What's Your Move?

"When you pass through the waters,
I will be with you; and when you pass through the rivers,
they will not sweep over you. When you walk
through the fire, you will not be burned."

—ISAIAH 43:2

I'm a little sad as I write this. I just found out a good friend is moving. Yet while I'm sad, I know she is the one feeling unnerved. New job, new town, new schools, new church, even a new set of friends. All that newness can stir up a lot of anxiety.

Even "little" moves can unsettle us: a promotion at work or a career change, moving deeper in a relationship, agreeing to serve at church, and so on. We find ourselves wondering, *What is going to happen?*

Whatever move we face—wherever we may be going— as believers, we have a constant traveling companion who promises to be with us in even the most dire circumstances.

We can never truly know everything that waits around the next corner. But we can be assured that God and His promises will be there to greet us.

What kind of move or change is leaving you feeling a bit unsettled today? Look closely: Do you see God there, waiting to make you feel at home?

Attention, Please!

I have fought the good fight, I have finished the race,
I have kept the faith.

—2 TIMOTHY 4:7

I've found, as a believer in Christ, that I must ask God to help me each day to focus on His things and not on all this earthly stuff. He seeks my undivided attention in spite of the distractions, temptations, and stresses that lie waiting around the next corner or the next news broadcast—and for a good reason. He knows He is more than enough in every area of my life.

Perhaps today is the time to rekindle your relationship with God. He is tugging at your heart, calling you, always inviting you to His plan of great purpose and abundance. He has written a new ending for your life in which Jesus says, "Well done, my good and faithful servant." That statement will be for all of us who took the time each day to get to know Him, love Him, and then obediently follow Him.

Help me, Lord, to pay attention to you so I can fight a good fight and finish well.

Blessed Assurance

Faith is confidence in what we hope for
and assurance about what we do not see.

—HEBREWS 11:1

"This is my story, this is my song,
Praising my Savior all the day long!"

This old hymn comes to my mind as I look back on my life. God was there even when I didn't realize it. God was there even when I didn't want Him to be! And God is with you … right now. He is helping you to write your story and your song. Call upon Him for whatever you need: strength, understanding, patience, wisdom. You have access to His infinite power.

I pray these words are like a big hug of encouragement to you right now: You are loved by this amazing God—how's that for a reason to give praise "all the day long"?

Set a timer on your watch (or computer or whatever gadget you prefer) to alert you at the beginning of each hour today. When you hear the beep, that's your cue to praise your Savior. By bedtime, you will truly have praised Him "all the day long."

No Flapping Required

Those who hope in the LORD will renew their strength.
They will soar on wings like eagles.

—ISAIAH 40:31

When hope is weak, we tend to flap our wings a lot. Have you noticed that? But Isaiah tells us that when our hope is properly focused, we will soar like eagles.

Soaring eagles rely on updrafts to lift them high, help them glide (no flapping required), and give them a wider perspective. When you've lost hope, isn't a wider perspective what you long for? Weariness comes when every ounce of our strength is so focused on the hope-robbing circumstance or person or memory that we can't see anything else. We desperately need a bird's-eye view that sees and believes that God is good and in control.

Ask God to lift you today on the updraft of His love and open your eyes to what He is doing in and through you.

Dream Bigger

"I have come that they may have life,
and have it to the full."

—JOHN 10:10

We all have dreams, don't we? We all feel there is more inside of us yet to be discovered. Do you dream of having more confidence? Of being able to transform a blank sheet of paper into a best seller? Of finding a place to fit in? Our dreams are as unique and varied as we are.

But when our dreams remain out of reach, we lose hope. We ditch the piano lessons, drop the workout sessions, and settle for what's more attainable. There's another way, however, of looking at unrealized dreams. They could be God's whispered invitation to move beyond our small dreams and into His big dream for us. Even when we find ourselves in good places in life, God is always inviting us to more, *to abundance*.

Don't stop dreaming! Surrender to God's dream for you—and believe it is beyond anything you could have imagined.

Is Your God Able?

"I do believe; help me overcome my unbelief!"

—MARK 9:24

Mary and Martha sent an urgent message to Jesus: Their brother was dying. But by the time Jesus arrived, Lazarus had died. Yet Jesus was well aware of the circumstances. He had already told His disciples, "Lazarus is dead, and for your sake I am glad I was not there, so that you may believe" (John 11:14–15).

He entered the situation knowing exactly what He was going to do. He enters your situation today in the same way. You may think He is too late, but He is right on time. Even though you feel overlooked or forgotten, He is about to bring great gain to you.

Martha responded to Jesus, "Yes, Lord ... I believe ..." (v. 27). How do you respond to Him?

Tell God about the "impossibilities" in your life that you are struggling to entrust to Him. Be honest with Him about your doubts and unbelief, like the father was who spoke the above words from Mark 9. Then let God speak words of courage to your heart. In conversations like this, your unbelief will steadily transform itself to belief.

Safe and Secure

He who watches over Israel
will neither slumber nor sleep.

—PSALM 121:4

Do you feel threatened by the evening news? Does the economy or the crime rate keep you awake at night with a sense that everything is spinning out of control?

When the children of Israel were troubled, God always showed up to remind them that He created this world and all that is in it. Psalm 78 recounts how God performed miracles in the land of Egypt. He parted the Red Sea and led them through. And He "guided them with the cloud by day and with light from the fire all night" (vv. 12–14). If He could do that, could there be any danger so great that He could not protect His creation from it?

What was true for the Israelites is true for us today. God still has the power to protect us, and still promises to do so.

Today, read the rest of Psalm 121 and let the words of the ancient psalmist set you free from fear.

The Lens of Faith

Faith is confidence in what we hope for
and assurance about what we do not see.

—HEBREWS 11:1

Faith does not mean we deny the burden we carry. It's just the opposite.

Faith gives us the courage and hope to confront our burden—painful, discouraging, even devastating as it is—with the promises as to *what it can be*: a blessing. Faith is the pair of glasses we use to see beyond the impossibility of the situation to the assurance that the impossible is already accomplished.

Put on your "faith glasses" today, then ask God to help you see the burdens in your life as the blessings He is already transforming.

A Taste of Freedom

The LORD has anointed me to …
proclaim freedom for the captives.
—ISAIAH 61:1

Look around you. Who looks weary? Worried? Who has a broken heart?

If we're honest, most of us do. Life takes us captive, wearing us down, filling us with doubt and shrinking confidence, robbing us of what and whom we love most. But that's not the end of the story. God anointed Jesus, His Son, to proclaim freedom for the captives. He gives to us who follow Jesus the same calling.

So ask yourself: *Who needs a taste of freedom today?*

All those words of encouragement that God has given you, all those promises—you get to pass them along to others. You get to spread the good news that He loves us and sets us free. You get to tell the hopeless that there's hope.

Among your friends and family members—even your enemies—who is weary or worried or brokenhearted? What is a practical way you can proclaim freedom to them today?

Dirt Busters

Let us draw near to God with a sincere heart and with
the full assurance that faith brings, having our hearts
sprinkled to cleanse us from a guilty conscience
and having our bodies washed with pure water.

—HEBREWS 10:22

A young woman who was a nurse lived with us for a time.
When she came home from the hospital, she would take
off her shoes in the garage. Then she would head straight to
the laundry room where she'd put all her clothes in the washing machine. Then she would jump in the shower and clean
herself from head to toe. She didn't want to bring any of the
contamination and bacteria from the hospital into our home.

Everything we come into contact with attaches itself to us
to some degree. So we come "home" to our Father for detox.
For cleansing. He doesn't say, "Shame on you for getting so
dirty." He says, "Come in, let me clean you up. Let's get all
that dirt off of you."

*Today, Lord, I come to you in sincerity and faith. Cleanse me
from guilt and wash me with your living water.*

Invisible Lights

I thank my God every time I remember you.
—PHILIPPIANS 1:3

The biggest robbers of our hope can be people. Do I hear an amen? But get this: The biggest *givers* of hope can also be people. The problem is they're often the people we don't pay much attention to. A hope giver could be … the barista who gives you a big smile at the coffee shop … the driver who waves you over when you're stuck in the wrong traffic lane … the men who pick up your trash (imagine if they didn't show up each week!).

When I walk through my day with this perspective, I begin to see brief yet beautiful twinkles of light all around me, like lightning bugs on a summer night. Your day will be so much brighter when you take time to notice those who bring light into your life.

Challenge yourself to notice the hope givers in your life today.

When Weak Is Strong

"My grace is sufficient for you, for my power
is made perfect in weakness."
—2 CORINTHIANS 12:9

You know those things you consider so imperfect about yourself? Here's the amazing news: God is waiting for you to hand them over so He can use them to fulfill His perfect plan for you! Did you get that? He wants your imperfections, not your perfection. It is through our weakness, the apostle Paul said, that God demonstrates His power. And that power can make miracles happen around us every day, even though we aren't perfect yet.

Read all of 2 Corinthians 12 so you can chew on these powerful truths about God's grace and power!

Controlled Chaos

You will keep in perfect peace those whose minds
are steadfast, because they trust in you.

—ISAIAH 26:3

The week had started off like any other. But then a pain in my husband's chest sent us by ambulance to Johns Hopkins Hospital. The speed at which we were traveling underlined my sense of how rapidly life was spinning out of control.

But *whose* control?

Later, while Lee rested in his room, I wandered the halls of Hopkins. In the rotunda I encountered a ten-foot marble statue of Jesus. The likeness was not real, but it brought a very real truth to my rescue: that my peace resides in the fact that the God I serve isn't pacing heaven's floor wondering how to handle the events of this day. He is in control even when I am not.

I am thankful that the week ended with a manageable diagnosis. But for many of you, life is far from manageable. I remind you that though you might often feel out of control, God promises to bring calm to your chaos.

Your circumstances may not change, but you will change from your encounters with the God of your circumstances. Take a moment to thank God for this wonderful assurance.

Three Reasons It's a Good Day

> While Jeremiah was still confined in the courtyard
> of the guard, the word of the LORD came to him a second
> time: "This is what the LORD says, he who made the earth,
> the LORD who formed it and established it—the LORD is his
> name: 'Call to me and I will answer you and tell you great
> and unsearchable things you do not know.'"
>
> —JEREMIAH 33:1–3

I hope you will take away three things from this wonderful passage of Scripture.

First, "the word of the Lord came to him a second time." That tells me that God does not give up on us. Even if it takes three, four, more times—and that also goes for your child that you worry about so much.

Second, God has amazing credentials: "He who made the earth … who formed it and established it." A God like that has the power to back up His promises!

And third, one of those promises is: "Call to me and I will answer you and tell you great and unsearchable things you do not know."

God listens intently for you to call on Him with even a whisper for help, advice, strength, or love. And He promises to answer! When He answers He will tell you things only He knows about your life. What a promise! What a promise keeper!

What is the Lord showing you and telling you today?

The Truth of the Matter

If our heart condemns us, God is greater than our heart,
and knows all things.

—I JOHN 3:20

've been thinking about an uncomfortable area where many
of us do silent battle: the area of insecurity or unworthiness.
When we strive to be all that God wants us to be, our enemy
will attack our thought life with little reminders of how far
short we fall and how much we lack.

The truth is that the belittling voices that make us feel
unworthy are *never* from God. God never condemns. He
always cheers us on and tells us to keep pressing ahead. He
tells us never to give up. He will restore us, strengthen us, and
make us steadfast (1 Peter 5:10).

No matter what the enemy says about us, God knows
us through and through, and He proclaims we are not only
good; we are *very* good. He promises that whatever He calls
us to, He will finish that good work.

*All-knowing God, help me move ahead, even when my heart
condemns me.*

Sprinkle Your World

"You are the salt of the earth."
—MATTHEW 5:13

I've read Matthew 5:13 more times than I can count. I was sure the truth of the verse had thoroughly sunk into my mind. But this week I read it differently: "You *are* the salt of the earth." Not "I hope you will be salt" but "You *are* salt." A fact.

Now, one thing I know about salt is that it is only useful as it is poured out. It can serve its purpose only as it comes into direct contact with something else. Suddenly a verse I thought I could skip over was giving me new encouragement. I *am* seasoning my world as I share my love of Christ; I *am* preserving the hopes and dreams of others as I share God's promises.

And you also *are* being used more than you can even imagine. I'm so thankful I stopped on that familiar verse this week so I could sprinkle some encouragement your way as well.

Besides being "the salt of the earth" (v. 13), what else does Jesus say about who you are (v. 14)?

Courage in the Storm

"Take courage! For I believe God.
It will be just as he said."

—ACTS 27:25 NLT

Some things are too much out of my control for comfort. If there's a task I can do alone, my attitude is "let me at it!" But when circumstances take me beyond my power to execute the plan, Kim can get *nervous*!

At those times, I have learned to recall Paul's words. During a violent storm, as others worried about being shipwrecked, Paul stood against worry and declared, "Take courage! For I believe God. It will be just as he said."

Our courage to stand in the storms of life also rests in what God has said. Even though those around you may claim the ship is going down, think back to what *God* has said. That's the truth in which you can stand.

What is the storm beyond your control today? In the midst of the wind and waves, take courage in the Lord.

Doing the Integrity Walk

He who walks in integrity walks securely,
but he who perverts his ways will be found out.

—PROVERBS 10:9 NASB

When I think of integrity, I think of Coach Cleveland Stroud of the Bulldogs of Conyers, Georgia. After his team's dramatic, come-from-behind state championship win, the coach voluntarily released information that stripped his team of the trophy. He had used an ineligible player for 45 seconds in the game.

This information would probably never have been uncovered. No one else seems to have been aware of it. Many saw the coach's disclosure as foolish.

But people of integrity are not fools. On the contrary, integrity is a quality of the wise, who prefer to walk through life being the same on the outside and the inside. Nothing to be "found out," because it's already "out there" for all to see. Long after most people will have forgotten the score of that game, they will remember Coach Stroud for his walk of integrity.

How can you walk in greater integrity today? If you're not sure, ask God to show you.

November

Popularity or Progress?

Do not conform any longer to the pattern of this world,
but be transformed by the renewing of your mind.

—ROMANS 12:2

It's human to want to be liked and accepted. Look at how much energy and angst goes into gathering Facebook friends and Twitter followers.

However, God isn't concerned about our popularity; neither does He want us to be. There's a fine line between "fitting in" and conforming to the "pattern of this world." God is concerned with our spiritual progress. If we want to stand out in the best possible way, it won't be by following the crowd; it will be by following in the footsteps of God's Son.

What are some ways that walking with God has helped you conform less to the world?

Need a Jumpstart?

Faith by itself,
if it is not accompanied by action, is dead.
—JAMES 2:17

Do you know what stops me in my tracks? Failure. Oh, for a while I might soldier on, looking good, going to Bible study, helping with the kids' program at church. But before long, my faith starts to sputter and stall.

And when my faith stalls, so does my activity, until I reach a state of near paralysis. That's when I need a jumpstart. A good friend helps—someone who will challenge what I say I believe about failure versus the way I act about my failure. Doing something for someone else helps because it takes my eyes off myself and shuts down my pity party. Talking to God helps too, because He always reminds me (when I'm willing to hear it) that my failure is not a reflection of who I am. He loves me just as much as when I was gliding along.

Like so much of our walk with God, the path through failure is a perfect combination of faith and action.

If failure stops you in your tracks this week, ask yourself three questions: Who can I call? Who can I help? What would God tell me right now about my sense of failure? Then take action.

Qualified by God

God chose the foolish things of the world
to shame the wise; God chose the weak things
of the world to shame the strong.

—1 CORINTHIANS 1:27

It was one of those days when I was feeling overwhelmed and underqualified for a task I believed God was calling me to do. All I could think about were my shortcomings. Yet I knew God was calling me to move forward. Then I came across the following paragraph, and it held the truths I needed to follow Him:

> Jacob was a cheater, Peter had a temper, David had an affair, Noah got drunk, Jonah ran from God, Paul was a murderer, Gideon was insecure, Miriam was a gossip, Martha was a worrier, Thomas was a doubter, Sarah was impatient, Elijah was depressed, Moses stuttered, Zaccheus was short, Abraham was old, and Lazarus was dead. *God doesn't always call the qualified, but He always qualifies the called.**

How much does that truth speak to you? Today, remind yourself that you don't have to be perfect for God to be active and at work in and through you.

---

* Anonymous, http://livingforjesus.com/god-doesnt-call-the-qualified-god-qualifies
-the-called/

The Power of Humility

Who is wise and understanding among you?
Let them show it by their good life,
by deeds done in humility that comes from wisdom.

—JAMES 3:13

I was blown away in our leadership team meeting. We had worked hard all morning—planning, seeking God's intentions. We each had our long to-do lists, but we each also had that good feeling that comes from making progress. Before we concluded, I asked for personal prayer requests. Without hesitation, one woman said, "Let's pray that *we* are the women God wants us to be, so that even before one Bible verse is spoken, all women who attend will see Jesus in *us*." The other women nodded in agreement. What a group!

James reminds us that the best demonstration of Christ in our life is our deeds. But not just any deeds. The deeds that really glorify God are those done through sincere humility.

Have you heard the old saying "Our lives may be the only Bible someone reads today"? Ask God to guide you to those who need to see Him through your humility today.

Hold That Growl!

Be kind and compassionate to one another,
forgiving each other, just as in Christ God forgave you.
—EPHESIANS 4:32

A lady "growled" at me today at the supermarket. My first impulse was to growl back. But then I looked at her and realized she's probably a lot like me. Maybe her new migraine meds make her feel jumpy and not quite herself. Maybe she said yes to too many things today and is now overwhelmed. Maybe someone just rammed into her cart and she felt the urge to take it out on someone else.

In the split second that all this ran through my mind, I chose not to growl back. A benefit of experiencing the ups and downs of life's journey is that we begin to judge less and empathize more. We realize we all carry around certain messes, and that realization can make us a little more compassionate, a little less judgmental, and a whole lot more accepting.

You can never know the hidden burdens a person is bearing. Keep that in mind if someone growls at you today.

Open Invitation

"Come to me, all you who are weary and burdened,
and I will give you rest."
—MATTHEW 11:28

Did you notice the simplicity of this invitation?

God doesn't say you must be Methodist, Catholic, Baptist, or Presbyterian. He doesn't say you must be young or old, creative or super-talented, extroverted or introverted. He doesn't even expect you to clean up first. Your heavenly Father simply says "come" to anyone who is weary and carrying too many burdens.

That's me. That's you. That's everyone who needs rest in body and soul.

Can you imagine a better invitation than that one? Come to Him today.

Wardrobe Woes

Put on the full armor of God.
—EPHESIANS 6:11

Figuring out what to wear can wear you out! We have to take into account what style and color suits us best, the weather conditions, whether casual or dressy is more appropriate, the fit of a garment—oh, and if we even like what's hanging in our closet (and if it's clean and ironed).

Well, as you might expect, God is much better at selecting what to wear than we are. The wardrobe He provides is good for all occasions, always in style, meets our needs, is one-size-fits-all, and is appropriate for all ages and lifestyles. In addition, it costs us nothing but provides us with everything we need to fight the battles that any given day brings to us.

Feeling insignificant?

Feeling unusable?

Feeling fearful?

Feeling dejected?

Feeling as if it's too late?

Feeling addicted?

Feeling alone?

God has the clothes to conquer all that.

Curious? Make time today to read Ephesians 6:10–17.
I guarantee, this is a wardrobe you will want to wear.

Performance Anxiety

The LORD makes firm the steps
of the one who delights in him.

—PSALM 37:23

Well, there I was. Again. Scratched and bleeding. Why had I run ahead? What was I thinking? What was *he* thinking? The tears began to stream down my face. I was overcome by the awful thought that I had disappointed the one I loved so dearly.

I knew those old roads on Top Street were full of potholes. That's one reason Granddad held my hand so securely on our walks. But this time I had let go of his hand to run ahead. I just wanted to show off a bit: how fast I could run, how I could dance as I ran, things like that. I forgot the road was not always smooth and safe. Down I went.

Granddad ran to where I lay. Then, he knelt beside me, and using his big hand, he lifted my face toward his. "You're OK," he whispered. "I'm here now." He wrapped me in his arms, lifted me up, and carried me home.

I so want to please you, heavenly Father. And sometimes I convince myself that the way to please you is to run and dance and "do." In a world where performance is priority, help me to grasp that I don't have to show off to please you, God.

Where's the Wisdom

If any of you lacks wisdom, you should ask God,
who gives generously to all without finding fault,
and it will be given to you.

—JAMES 1:5

Information is everywhere. Television commercials, billboards, magazine covers, Internet ads. They're all designed to make us feel like we're lacking something essential if we don't consume the information they are selling. James, on the other hand, tells us we have a source to go to any time we feel we lack information or understanding about an issue in our lives. And this Source will never make us feel condemned or inadequate. This Source—God—promises to give generously and freely. Now that, my friends, is my information center of choice!

In what area of your life do you seek wisdom today? God loves it when we ask His advice, so ask, and then listen carefully.

Spread the Hope

Praise be to the God and Father of our Lord Jesus Christ,
the Father of compassion and the God of all comfort,
who comforts us ..., so that we can comfort those ...
with the comfort we ourselves have received from God.

—2 CORINTHIANS 1:3–4

Are you overwhelmed by something that does not normally faze you? Are you feeling misunderstood? Do you feel sad for no apparent reason? Are you wondering if anything in your crazy schedule really matters?

May I invite you to stay in that place? Don't rush to get out of it before you have a chance to learn from it. In fact, I suggest you grab a pencil and take some notes. You see, I'm a firm believer that God equips and prepares us through the things we experience—including (maybe especially) the difficult things.

Today, turn your prayer inward. Write down what you are feeling. What emotions are swirling inside you? Then look in your Bible's concordance (index) for a soothing Scripture and allow God's words to comfort you. Next, thank God for the hope and comfort you have received from Him. And ask Him for the opportunity to pass along that hope and comfort to another person.

The Book of Treasures

All Scripture is God-breathed and is useful for teaching,
rebuking, correcting and training in righteousness.
—2 TIMOTHY 3:16

When Paul wrote his second letter to his protégé Timothy, he urged Timothy to consider what a treasure the Scriptures were.

First, the Bible is a treasure because it is God-breathed. We often speak of Shakespeare or Tolstoy as being inspired, but that is human inspiration mixed with a good dose of perspiration. The words I read in my Bible are from God Himself. No other book makes that claim.

Second, the Bible is a treasure because it is useful for every need we bring to it. Some books entertain, which helps us unwind after a stressful day. Others teach us a new skill or enlighten us about what it's like to live in another era or culture. Still others, often called self-help books, show us what we're doing wrong (in our diets, relationships, or careers) and how to do better.

And finally, God's Word is a treasure because it transforms us. When we dig among its treasures, we are "thoroughly equipped for every good work" (v. 17). In other words, we are equipped to be a treasure to someone else.

How has today's devotional prompted you to view your Bible differently?

Take Heart!

"In this world you will have trouble.
But take heart! I have overcome the world."
—JOHN 16:33

For years and years, I just wanted God to fix me. Do you ever feel like that: "Just fix everything that hurts, God. Wave your magic wand!" But He does something much better. He allows us to walk through the transformation with Him. And with each tiny step, He helps us replace the lies we've been telling ourselves with His truth. We don't need a magic wand when we have God's truth.

One of those truths is in John 16:33. We know all about trials and tribulations. Health issues, financial worries, loneliness, abuse, loss, rocky marriages, rebellious teenagers. We know life gets hard at times. But there's more to the story. Jesus says, *Take heart for I have overcome them.*

I didn't get that second part for a long time, but that's His promise. He's saying, "I'm bigger than anything that's in your bag of burdens." That's the truth we can cling to when we're facing things that could make us lose hope.

In the past, where have you searched for relief from your worries and burdens? Which fixes were effective in giving you long-lasting hope?

On the Lookout

"Whom shall I send, and who will go?"
—ISAIAH 6:8

Do you sometimes feel as if God has thrown up His hands in frustration and is allowing this old world to fall to pieces? The news headlines seem to indicate that, don't they?

But the Bible paints a different picture of God. Isaiah 6:8 describes the Lord's voice saying, "Whom shall I send, and who will go?" I imagine Him searching our homes, churches, communities, cities, and beyond, and asking, "Whom shall I send into this school or to the football games, into this department store or this laundry, into this neighborhood to live in this for-sale house?"

God still cares for this troubled world, and He is looking for someone to work in and through to display His glory and power. He doesn't need our talents or our plans. He simply wants our willing, obedient hearts. He will strengthen us, empower us, and equip us to accomplish His will so that the world can see that He loves them.

God, send me. I will go to this broken world and let You shine Your love through me.

A Worthy Truth

"The LORD your God is with you,
the Mighty Warrior who saves. He will take great delight
in you; in his love he will no longer rebuke you,
but will rejoice over you with singing."

—ZEPHANIAH 3:17

It gives me great joy today to tell you that your heart has caught God's eye.

He "gets" you.

He understands you.

He knows you through and through, and He loves you.

He is bigger than your condemning heart.

He finds you worthy.

He sees all you can be.

Carry that truth with you all day. It can change your life.

Search the Internet for the lyrics to "He Knows My Name" (be sure to include the quotes). You'll see the song was written by Tommy Walker and has been covered by bands like D.C. Talk. Compare with a single from Francesca Battistelli's album If We're Honest, also titled "He Knows My Name." How did the lyrics speak to your heart?

Lost: One Mind

God has not given us a spirit of fear, but of power
and of love and of a sound mind.

—2 TIMOTHY 1:7 NKJV

This morning I brewed my usual cup of coffee. As always, I put my coffee in the microwave to get it super warm while I grabbed my laptop. At least, that was my plan. But when I opened the microwave, the plan went awry. The coffee was gone! Was this a magic trick or was I losing my mind?

Later, I made a disturbing discovery. I had *not* put my fresh cup of coffee in the microwave; I had put it back in the cabinet with the clean mugs. Have you ever done anything like this? Please tell me you have!

I must admit, such lapses once caused me trepidation. But now I realize most of us simply have way too much on our minds. So, rather than believing we're losing our minds, let's choose to believe in the minds God has given each of us today.

All day today, whatever happens, declare with a big smile, "But I have a sound mind!"

Against All Hope

Against all hope, Abraham in hope believed and
so became the father of many nations.

—ROMANS 4:18

Abraham put his trust in God against all hope. He was
old, and his wife was barren, yet God had promised him
offspring beyond count.

Where does that kind of hope come from? I believe
Romans 4:21 holds the answer: Abraham was "fully per-
suaded that God had power to do what he had promised."
Hope and faith are inseparable.

The same God who made Abraham a father of nations
offers His power to you today. Set aside your notion of what
can't be done. God is able (and eager!) to act with power in
your life too.

*What seems dead to you today? Your marriage? Your dreams?
What seems too large to conquer? Your depression? Your
anger? A stubborn habit? Against all hope, believe!*

What I Love about Conversations

A person finds joy in giving an apt reply—
and how good is a timely word!
—PROVERBS 15:23

A cup of coffee and heart-to-heart talk with a friend is about as good as it can get. One of my favorite topics of conversation is whatever God happens to be teaching me at any given moment. You see, I like having conversations with Him too.

A recurring conversation I have with God centers around this great truth: the burdens we bear today can become, in God's hands, the blessings of tomorrow. This has become my life message.

The best conversations are with women who are willing to risk being real. When we "just talk" in a safe place, among like-hearted women, we receive wisdom and courage and hope for the hour or day or week ahead of us.

And finally, what I love about conversations is that you can enjoy them in your PJs or your pearls!

What do you love about conversations?

Hurry Up and Stop

"Be still, and know that I am God."
—PSALM 46:10

I've learned that when I'm the busiest, that's when I need to stop in my tracks. When I'm the most rushed and crazed is when I most need to reexamine my priorities. Am I focused on what seems *important* and missing what is truly *needed*?

The story of Mary and Martha reminds me of the difference. Their story in Luke 10:38–42 shows Martha busy with what she saw as important and upset with Mary for "just" sitting at the Lord's feet. Jesus responded to Martha this way: "Martha, Martha, you are worried and upset about many things, but few things are needed—or indeed only one. Mary has chosen what is better" (vv. 41–42).

I have been placed on this earth for a reason. I don't want to be so busy for the sake of being busy that I lose sight of why I am here and what is genuinely *needed*.

Are you crazy busy? It's sure easy to get that way! You may want to take an inventory of your schedule this week. What is creating the busyness in your life? What is really needed?

The Past Is Past

"The former things have taken place,
and new things I declare."

—ISAIAH 42:9

When I read these words that God spoke through His prophet Isaiah, it's as if God is saying to me today, "I know all about your past. It is done. The past is history; that is where it needs to remain—in the past. I'm going to do something new."

How amazing is that! He knows my past—every mistake, regret, doubt, how I was abused, and how I abused—and He still finds me worthy.

Let the hope of these words flow over you for a moment. Then call someone who needs a good dose of hope, and tell her this great truth.

What a Masterpiece!

We are God's [masterpiece],
created in Christ Jesus to do good works,
which God prepared in advance for us to do.

—EPHESIANS 2:10

One day a sculptor was working on a huge rock with his hammer and chisel. A man came along and asked with a smirk, "Why are you wasting your time on that ugly rock?" The sculptor replied, "I see a beautiful angel trapped in this rock, and I'm doing my best to let him out."

When others looked at Simon the fisherman, they saw an opinionated, self-centered hothead. But God knew He could chisel out of the rough rock named Simon a great man who would become Peter. And only the Lord could see beyond the fearful, excuse-making Gideon to His future "mighty warrior."

Do you know what your Master Artist sees when He looks at you today? Someone even you cannot see or imagine! God chooses you as you *are*—but He also sees you as you *will be*. Man judges and chooses based on outer appearances, but God has chosen you because He sees your heart for Him.

If you awoke today feeling like an ugly rock, then let Ephesians 2:10 remind you that God has put more into you and sees more in you than you can imagine.

That's What Friends Are For

Two are better than one,
because they have a good return for their labor.

—ECCLESIASTES 4:9

En route to one of our son's college football games, Lee and I scooted into a service station for a quick fill-up.

Nearby, a car with obvious mechanical problems sputtered to a grinding stop at a busy exit. After several failed attempts to restart the car, a man jumped out and, with the door open and one hand on the steering wheel, tried single-handedly to push the vehicle out of the way of traffic. I saw little heads bobbing in the back seat.

Before I could call out to Lee to help, another car came to a stop. That driver jumped out and began to push the disabled car. Then another car pulled over, and another driver joined in the pushing. Next two men ran out from a nearby store and added their muscle power.

We all stall at times. That's life. The next time I stall, I want friends like those I saw along that roadside.

Lord, I want to be that kind of friend to those around me who stall. A friend who simply sees a need and responds to it.

A Thanksgiving Tradition

We ought always to thank God for you,
brothers and sisters, and rightly so, because your faith
is growing more and more, and the love all of you
have for one another is increasing.

—2 THESSALONIANS 1:3

I love Thanksgiving. I love the cooking, the grand desserts, the nap that always follows. But even more, I love that it's a day set aside to appreciate the people and things we value. Several years ago I started a new tradition in our family to make it easier to express how much we value one other.

As my house filled with loved ones, I wrote each person's name on a slip of paper, folded the slips, and put them a basket. Once we were seated, I passed the basket around. Everybody took a name, read it, but kept it confidential. Then I asked everyone to think of (1) something they loved about the person on their slip, or (2) a special memory involving that person.

The outcome was beyond wonderful! Some stories had us laughing; others left us in awe as we learned things we didn't know about each other. Through our Thanksgiving traditions, our children (and eventually our grandchildren) discover how the people they know and love have walked through life with faith and godly character.

What new tradition would you like to start this Thanksgiving?

Stuck in the Right Place

Always be joyful. Never stop praying.
Be thankful in all circumstances, for this is God's will
for you who belong to Christ Jesus.
—1 THESSALONIANS 5:16–18 NLT

I can't stop thinking this morning about the many challenges my friends face: chemotherapy, a troubled teen, work stress, and job loss. And then there are the "ordinary" challenges: how to be a better friend, how to be kinder to a spouse, how to juggle competing time demands. You know what I'm talking about.

How would God tell us to begin a day like this? His answer may seem more difficult than our circumstances: Be joyful, pray, and give thanks! Are you shaking your head in disbelief, finding it hard to be the tiniest bit joyful? Does it seem impossible to offer even a syllable of thanks? Then I suppose you are stuck.

But that's not a bad place to be. For when you are stuck between joy and thanksgiving, it means you are praying, and that means you are right in the middle of God's will. Be joyful, *never stop praying*, and be thankful.

When we're burdened with the weight of life's challenges, prayer is a tremendous gift. So let God know about your friends who need burdens lifted today. Let Him know about the burdens you carry this day. Wait ... what's that? Could it be joy?

The Power of Thankfulness

> Then they took the stone away and Jesus raised his eyes
> and said, "Father, I thank you that you have heard me."
>
> —JOHN 11:41 PHILLIPS

I've always loved the praise and worship segment of a church service. But my boys—not so much. Sunday after Sunday, I'd nudge and elbow to encourage them to participate. Finally one of my guys looked at me and said, "We may not be singing on the outside, Mom, but we are singing in our hearts."

For many people, thankfulness and praise do not flow easily. Perhaps you're uncomfortable with expressing yourself in song. Maybe you simply can't find much to be thankful for.

This was the case with Mary and Martha. At the tomb of Lazarus, we see these sisters spewing their disappointment to Jesus. But Jesus tells them, that Lazarus will live if they will believe. And next He does something surprising to bring life in the face of death. He looks up. Then He gives thanks.

Jesus has brought you to the place of your next miracle. And you can unleash God's miracle-making power today by believing and by proclaiming your thanksgiving.

Look up today! If nothing else, you can be thankful God hears you. "This is the confidence we have in approaching God: … he hears us" (1 John 5:14).

Living Wisdom

[Wisdom] is a tree of life to those who take hold of her;
those who hold her fast will be blessed.

—PROVERBS 3:18

As we grow in wisdom, we become life givers. It's a naturally flowing process. We seek wisdom from God through His Word. That wisdom grows slowly and steadily within us and then begins to flow outward from us. And where does it flow? To people in need of life—abundant life, everlasting life.

As we fill our hearts with God's wisdom, we speak life to those around us. That's an awesome responsibility and opportunity that God has given us. It gives us significance wherever we go.

Bless me, Lord, with the gift of wisdom. Transform my heart, so my words bring life to those around me.

What Next, God?

"Stop at the crossroads and look around. Ask for the old,
godly way, and walk in it. Travel its path,
and you will find rest for your souls."
—JEREMIAH 6:16 NLT

Who among us hasn't felt a bit confused and lost and even doubtful when it comes to knowing what God would have us do next? Sometimes the practical, everyday decisions in life help us understand the more intangible spiritual decisions we face. For example, if I were on a road trip and got lost, what would I do? I would find a safe place to stop and ask for directions.

That's why, when I am seeking God's direction, I follow the Jeremiah 6:16 path: I pause, ponder, pray, and then proceed.

I pause. "Stop," the verse says. That means I carry on with life, but I don't make a spiritual step toward whatever I'm not sure about.

I ponder. What is the "crossroad"? What is the decision to be made, and what are my choices?

I pray. I "ask" because God promises that if I ask, He will answer with wisdom I don't yet know (Jeremiah 33:3).

I proceed. I walk the path God shows me.

How might the process outlined in Jeremiah 6:16 work itself out in your life?

Still Higher

I lift up my eyes to the mountains—where does
my help come from? My help comes from the LORD,
the Maker of heaven and earth.

—PSALM 121:1–2

Mountains are inspiring! We look up, and the troubles
threatening to overcome us at low altitude seem a bit
less significant. We feel a whisper of hope.

But is a whisper enough?

The writer of Psalm 121 points us to a more certain source
of hope. He looks to the mountains and tells himself: *No,
these mountains aren't the source of my help. So where does my
help come from?* Immediately he gives us his conclusion: *My
help comes the Lord, the Maker of heaven and earth.*

Day after day, we face moments when we look about for
help. The world offers all kinds of counterfeit sources of help,
some of them effective for a time. But why settle for the thing
that was made (the mountains) when you can get help from
the Maker?

*Jesus says to you today, "Look higher! Look at Me! I'm where
your help comes from. I'm where your hope comes from."
What are you going to say to Him in response?*

Expect the Unexpected

"We will give our attention to prayer
and the ministry of the word."

—ACTS 6:4

If you are like me, then just as you begin your prayer time a zillion things starting fighting for your attention. The laundry buzzer goes off, your phone rings, the dog starts chewing the rug. You get the picture, right?

Rather than getting frustrated, I decided long ago to begin my prayers whether or not the environment was perfect. Part of my preparation is to expect the unexpected. That way the interruptions are just that—interruptions—and not prayer-time stealers.

What are your most common distractions during prayer?
Brainstorm with a friend some practical solutions.

The Gift of Attention

Each one will be like a shelter from the wind
and a refuge from the storm.

—ISAIAH 32:2

A little boy kept running away from home. He did this so often that the police knew exactly which neighbor's home to go to when seeking the young runaway.

After several such occurrences, a police officer asked the boy, "Why do you keep running away to the same lady's house?"

With his head bowed low and with a sheepish voice, the boy responded, "She never looks at her watch when I'm talking to her."

Who needs your undivided attention today? Yes, it's a busy, busy season, but can you find a few spare moments to let someone just talk?

Broken Prizes

I have become like broken pottery.

—PSALM 31:12

When Trey, my oldest, was little, he delighted in buying small pottery pieces for me. Especially angels. Yet he would often present them to me with tears of frustration. You see, in his excitement to get his special "prize" (that's what he called his gifts) to me, Trey would unfailingly drop, bang, or otherwise break it. But he was so determined to present his gift that he would give it to me anyway.

To sooth his feelings, I would hold the gift in my hands and say, "But Trey, this makes it so special. No one else has one just like the one you are giving Mommy." A big smile would break through the tears, and he would jump in my arms for a hug.

When I feel most broken, it helps me to recall how precious my glued angels are to me. God feels the same about us today. He sees our brokenness, but He delights in our courage to present ourselves to Him just as we are.

In God's eyes we are His prize; our chips, cracks, and bumps just makes us more special in our Potter's hand.

December

Anticipating Christmas

Forgetting what is behind …
—PHILIPPIANS 3:13

Can you believe it's December? Are you wondering where the year went?

The beginning of a new month can trigger a rush of guilt and regret over all the things we meant to do and didn't. And December may be the worst month of all because, in addition to all we didn't quite get done in the previous eleven months, we now have a mile-long Christmas to-do list staring us in the face.

But I propose another way to enter into this month. What if we forget what is behind us, and gaze with anticipation at what lies ahead? What if, amid the holiday mayhem, we decorate ourselves with the wonder of Christmas? How? By giving ourselves a Christmas gift of three minutes, five minutes, maybe ten whole minutes each day to sip some coffee, read a short devotional or Bible passage, and let the love and peace of God fill our anxious, striving hearts. We may end up enjoying our best Christmas ever.

Take a minute to identify one thing about this month that fills you with wonder and joy. Is it an upcoming event? A person you'll see soon? A particular gift you can't wait to buy?

Purposed Heart

> But Daniel purposed in his heart …
> —DANIEL 1:8 KJV

December is most likely your busiest month of the year. To your regular workload, you will add school plays, social functions at work, sending Christmas cards, buying and wrapping gifts, and …

Would you like me to stop now? The big question is how will you do all this and still enjoy the season? Daniel shows the way. Before his values and priorities were challenged by circumstances, he "purposed in his heart" not to be swayed from his convictions.

Ask God to help you be true to the Christmas values He has placed in your heart too.

Today, identify what you want this Christmas to mean to you and your family. Then look at your schedule: Which activities contribute to your Christmas values? What activities have you added to your schedule that aren't all that important and will interfere with celebrating Christmas the way your heart wants to?

A Child's Faith

No matter how many promises God has made,
they are "Yes" in Christ.

—2 CORINTHIANS 1:20

Adults struggle with believing promises. A child doesn't. When I was little, someone told me that if I circled what I wanted in the Sears catalog, Santa would bring me everything I wished for. That same person told me that most people think Santa only comes once a year at Christmas, but for a few very special people who knew this secret, he comes more often. And I believed those wonderful promises.

In my case, the person making the promises wasn't trustworthy. After a few experiences like mine, children grow into distrustful adults. But where God's promises are concerned, we need to revert to our childlike trust. With God, we can be certain of the outcome. The timing may not match what we had in mind, but He always keeps His promises.

Like so much in life, childlike trust takes practice. The more I receive from God, the more my confidence in Him grows. I'm learning to filter out the lies that say, "He's not going to do that for you," and instead to focus on what I know is true about His character.

When you present your prayer requests to God today, simply ask, like a child who is certain of her Father's promises.

Baggage Check

Cast all your anxiety on him because he cares for you.

—I PETER 5:7

Will you be in an airport this Christmas?

If so, watch the travelers as they enter with their heavy loads. Notice them dragging large suitcases, carrying medium ones, wrapping smaller ones around their shoulders and even necks. They grunt, sweat, tug, and maneuver with one goal in mind: the check-in counter.

Once they've exchanged their heavy luggage for a weightless boarding pass, they emerge as different people: smiling, unencumbered, and ready to enjoy the journey.

What baggage weighs you down today? What load is preventing you from enjoying this season? Jesus urges you to check your bags with Him today.

Who Do You Say I Am?

> "What about you? …
> Who do you say I am?"
> —LUKE 9:20

O nce when Jesus was praying in private and his disciples were with him, he asked them, "Who do the crowds say I am?"

"They replied, 'Some say John the Baptist; others say Elijah; and still others, that one of the prophets of long ago has come back to life.'

'But what about you?' he asked. 'Who do you say I am?'

Peter answered, 'God's Messiah.' (Luke 9:18–21)

The angels, the crowds, the followers, and the religious elite—they all had many names for Jesus, many titles. But for each of us, Jesus makes it personal. "What about you?" He asks. "Who do you say I am?"

Let the answer to Jesus' question be your Christmas meditation today. Then tell someone else who Jesus is to you.

Peer Pressured

God is faithful; he will not let you be tempted
beyond what you can bear. But when you are tempted,
he will also provide a way out so that you can endure it.

—1 CORINTHIANS 10:13

In December, the pressure of the crowd is especially powerful. Television advertisements entice you to spend beyond your means. Social functions dazzle you with decadent desserts. Office parties wink at your personal standards and whisper, *Lower them just this once. It's Christmas!* What do you do amid this onslaught of temptations to overspend, overindulge, and overcompromise?

As you face temptations, remember that being tempted is not wrong. A temptation is merely an invitation—you can accept it and do what Satan (often disguised as "the crowd") wants you to do, or you can refuse it and do what God wants you to do. Temptation never forces us to give in; God always provides a way out.

Today when you face one of the season's temptations, just relax, pray for strength, and say no to the invitation.

Dot to Dot

[Stand] firm in the faith, because you know that
the family of believers throughout the world
is undergoing the same kind of sufferings.

—1 PETER 5:9

God doesn't sugarcoat anything. While we may buy into
the myth that accepting Christ means an easy, problem-free, happy life, that is just not true.

What is true? That we have an everlasting relationship
and an eternal glory in Christ.

Do you find it hard to picture *everlasting* and *eternal?* Imagine a dot—your earthly life. From that dot, begin to draw a
line. Continue that line around the globe ... and around the
globe again ... and again, again, and again. That line is just
the beginning of eternity and the eternal glory you've been
promised.

*For now, you may suffer, but it won't always be so. Take
time to give thanks that the God of all grace is—at this
moment, even as you struggle—working out His plan for your
eternal gain.*

Please Pass the Comfort

We can comfort those in any trouble
with the comfort we ourselves receive from God.
—2 CORINTHIANS 1:4

My garage is packed, my pantry is filled, and my closet overflows. I need to give some things away!

The same can be said of my heart today. I have a clutter of stored hurts and pains. I also have incredible stories of how God's promises have gotten me through. Just as I need to give away some of my material blessings, perhaps I should give away more of my stories of hope. I need to comfort others with the ways God has comforted me.

What hope have you already received from God? Look into your heart of stored comfort today and pass along a bit of that comfort to someone God puts on your mind or along your path.

Christmas Contentment

I have learned the secret of being content
in any and every situation.
—PHILIPPIANS 4:12

This is a hard time of year for practicing contentment, isn't it? It feels as if there's never enough money to purchase the gifts you really want to give, the decorations, the seasonal goodies, and those cute party shoes. And I suspect you also wish you had more money to give to all those great charities that surface at Christmas.

Paul learned the secret to contentment. He chose to focus on being who God wanted Him to be, and doing what God showed him to do, instead of on what he had or did not have.

That probably sounds like a tall order right now. But doesn't it sound a lot better than being mired in frustration and discontent?

You can't muster up contentment on your own, but you can discover it with God's help. So call on Him today, "whether well fed or hungry, whether living in plenty or in want" (v. 12)!

Great Expectations

"If you then, though you are evil, know how to give good
gifts to your children, how much more will your Father in
heaven give good gifts to those who ask him!"

—LUKE 11:13

When the boys were little, I would yell at Lee, "You'd better get the camcorder out, because I'm waking up the boys!" (It was usually about 4 a.m.) Here's why I was so excited: Months earlier the boys had made their Christmas lists, and now their dreams were (mostly) going to come true.

Well, that's the good side of Christmas. Do you know the bummer side? We have to wait until Christmas to give our kids these gifts! Right? It was the worst thing for me to know that I had bought and hidden away what was going to make their hearts happy, but I had to wait to give it to them.

God knows what we need. He knows what will delight our hearts. And all of it has been purchased and paid for by Him. We just have to wait on the right timing. Sometimes I think that's why God doesn't sleep. I think He's excited about giving us our blessings. His blessings are already here. They are already purchased. We just have to keep going until God says it's time.

*Can you recall a time when you struggled with waiting on
God for His timing? Once the anticipated "gift" arrived, how
did you feel? Do you know of someone who would benefit
from hearing about your experience? If so, tell them!*

Take the Burn out of Burnout

Never tire of doing what is right.

—2 THESSALONIANS 3:13

There's no time like Christmas for rolling up your sleeves and doing good deeds. Opportunities abound: visiting nursing homes, serving meals at soup kitchens, or delivering gifts to children in need. Are you getting tired just thinking about it?

Burnout is common at Christmas. Maybe you have learned how to pace yourself and protect your physical and emotional health. But all around you are people who are on overload at this time of year.

What can you do to encourage these people—your pastor, for instance, or your local first responders? A small act or simple word can go a long way. And you will benefit as well. Proverbs 11:25 tell us that "whoever refreshes others will be refreshed."

The Only Opinion That Matters

"He will take great delight in you."

—ZEPHANIAH 3:17

For years, nothing upset me more than if a relationship with a workmate, a ministry colleague, a good friend, or a family member seemed strained. I would worry, worry, worry about what I did wrong, how I might have disappointed those people, and what they might be saying about me. Sound familiar?

I've come to realize that to focus on what people are saying about me is to miss a much higher priority: a focus on what God has to say about me. So refocus. Forgive what needs to be forgiven. Forget ugly words. Turn your back on negativity. Instead, run into the open arms of God:

The one who calls you to purpose and significance (Jeremiah 1:5).

The one who says you are the apple of His eye (Zechariah 2:8).

The one who has chosen you to be His beloved child (Romans 8:15).

The one who is singing your praises today (Zephaniah 3:17).

Thank you, Lord, for taking delight in me. Help me walk through this day with the mental image of you singing my praises.

Monkey Business

God saw all that he had made, and it was very good.

—GENESIS 1:31

I need to remind myself daily that from the moment of creation, we were declared "very good." As if God had said to each of us at birth, "I love who you are, and I love what you are going to become."

Do you hear the space and freedom in those words, the love and acceptance? We're always going to be better on some days than others. Some days we'll shine, some days we'll droop, and some days we'll swing from trees … *What?* Maybe this story will explain what I mean. It comes from a mom I know.

"I talked with my boys about how the Bible says that people who do not complain and argue are like stars, shining brightly in the sky. We talked about what complaining and arguing is. Then I told them that when we don't do those things, God thinks we're so shiny we are like stars. Noah (age three) told me he doesn't want to be a star today. He just wants to be a monkey."

Are you feeling like a monkey today or a shining star? God knows you through and through, loves you unconditionally, and gives you the freedom to be a little monkey now and then. So feel free to swing a little.

Standing Trial

> Consider it pure joy … whenever you face trials
> of many kinds, because you know that the testing
> of your faith develops perseverance … so that you
> may be mature and complete.
>
> —JAMES 1:2–4

*B*ZZZZZZZ. *This is only a test.*

Are you familiar with this message on your TV or radio? It's a cautionary measure to ensure we have advance warning in case of a real emergency.

James gives us an "advance warning" in today's passage: Trials are coming! And then he goes a step further. He offers hope: These trials will mature and complete you.

Expect some trials this Christmas. An annoying family member. A trip to the emergency room. An overload of seasonal stress. These trials descend on us almost every December, don't they? Here's the difference: This year, we know the outcome of our trials. We will be more complete, more mature, more like the person God created us to be.

When you encounter "trials of many kinds" today, stand up taller and declare, "Never mind. I know the outcome, and it's a good one!"

Capture and Replace

Take captive every thought to make it obedient to Christ.

—2 CORINTHIANS 10:5

Doubt expresses itself in different ways. For me, it might say, *What's the use?* or *God doesn't care.* What's more, I put way too much pressure on myself with my unrealistic expectations. When I hear these and similar messages, I can "take captive" that thought and make it obedient to Christ by putting His truth to it. For example, if my thoughts tell me *God doesn't care,* I can remind myself of 1 Peter 5:7: "Cast all your anxiety on him because *he cares for you*" (emphasis mine). When doubt leaves me feeling lost and uncertain about what to do, I personalize the truth of James 1:5: If I lack wisdom, I should ask God and He will give generously.

Where is doubt nagging at you today? Capture that thought and replace it with a truth you're learning from your daily devotionals. Sometimes the simplest weapon is the mightiest: "Jesus loves me, this I know."

Whose Priority?

Jesus loved Martha and her sister and Lazarus.
Yet when he heard that Lazarus was sick, he stayed where
he was two more days, and then he said to his disciples,
"Let us go back to Judea."

—JOHN 11:5–7

How many activities did you add to this month's calendar because you didn't want to make someone angry? How many times did you say yes because you felt guilty saying no? What did you agree to do just because you've done it every other time you were asked?

Jesus was never pressured by others' priorities. He loved Martha and her family deeply, yet He didn't rush to their aid just to please them. His daily steps were determined by one priority: His desire to please His Father.

Who will determine your priorities today? Ask God to show you what needs to disappear from your calendar and to-do list. Ask Him if He wants you to add anything. Surrender your day to Him to use as He sees fit.

Sticky Friends

There is a friend who sticks closer than a brother.
—PROVERBS 18:24

Who has been there for you when no one else stuck around? Who has seen the worst in you and yet believed the best about you?

Mary needed a friend like that. She is believed to have been about fourteen years old when the angel Gabriel appeared to her and said, "Do not be afraid, Mary; you have found favor with God. You will conceive and give birth to a son, and you are to call him Jesus" (Luke 1:30–31). Pregnant and unmarried? She could lose everything: her reputation, her family, her beloved Joseph, her very life. Can you imagine how she felt? How afraid? How alone?

But wait! There's Elizabeth, her cousin. Elizabeth would not abandon her. As imperfect as Mary's situation was, Elizabeth was the perfect friend. During the three months that Mary stayed with her, I believe Elizabeth kept pointing Mary toward God's perfect plan for her.

Do you know someone in need of a "sticky" friend for a sticky situation? Don't wait for her to call you; call her today!

Putting on Approval

If anyone is in Christ, the new creation has come.
The old has gone, the new is here!

—2 CORINTHIANS 5:17

Just as we put on our clothes each morning, we should also put on God's approval. This may seem awkward at first, because the world we live in rarely sends us messages of approval. Total acceptance is not shouted from the billboards, gleaned from our magazines, or communicated in our daily conversations. Instead, we—and our culture—dwell on how we *don't* measure up. We condemn our flaws and belabor past failures.

The truth is, none of us has "arrived." We're all a work in progress in God's eyes! And we *have* made progress, believe me!

Stop for a moment and just be thankful that you are not what you used to be. Celebrate how far God has brought you today.

Do You Hear What I Hear?

A great and powerful wind tore the mountains apart …
but the LORD was not in the wind. After the wind there was
an earthquake, but the LORD was not in the earthquake.
After the earthquake came a fire, but the LORD was not in
the fire. And after the fire came a gentle whisper.

—1 KINGS 19:11–12

Where will you listen for the Lord today?

In the church choir? He might be there.

In the blare of the mall's Christmas marching band? He might be there also.

In the sigh of a weary waitress? He might be there as well.

Elijah expected God to speak to him in dramatic, impossible-to-miss ways, perhaps. But God didn't thunder down from heaven; He whispered.

How will God speak to you today? You never know. Be expectant. Be listening. Be ready to be surprised.

Unbelievable

"I know that you can do all things;
no purpose of yours can be thwarted."
—JOB 42:2

Many great men and women in the Bible had occasions when they could not figure out what God was up to. Abraham could not understand why God would ask him to give up what he loved most in the world, his son. Moses could not understand why God would keep him wandering in the wilderness for forty years. And dear Mary and Martha tried desperately to understand why Jesus lingered when their brother Lazarus was dying.

What in your life leaves you dumbfounded? What seems unfair? What do you long for that God seems to be withholding? Perhaps God has brought you to this place to prepare you for His next miracle in your life. The world proclaims, "You need to see to believe." But Jesus declares the opposite: "Believe, then you will see" (John 11:40, paraphrased).

Today, you may not understand your situation, but will you declare a renewed belief that, from that situation, God is preparing to call forth a miracle? It may be a miracle of healing or restoration; of strength or favor; of salvation or exoneration; of a job, forgiveness, patience, or kindness. Begin this day praying for and believing in your miracle.

A Christmas Legacy

I have been reminded of your sincere faith,
which first lived in your grandmother Lois and in
your mother Eunice and … now lives in you also.

—2 TIMOTHY 1:5

Billy Graham says, "The greatest legacy one can pass on to one's children and grandchildren is not money or other material things accumulated in one's life but rather a legacy of character and faith."

Never underestimate the far-reaching consequences of your influence on one child. Timothy is an example of that. His father was not a believer, but the godly influence of his mother and grandmother prevailed. So powerful was their influence that young Timothy encouraged the formidable Paul and still encourages us today.

Will you be among children this Christmas (or anyone who hasn't heard the good news)? If so, tell them how you met Jesus—not only as a baby in a manger but as a Savior and Lord and Friend.

Even If ...

"If we are thrown into the blazing furnace,
the God we serve is able to deliver us from it. ...
But even if he does not, ...we will not serve your gods."
—DANIEL 3:17–18

Will you still serve God "even if"? Even if you can't make your mortgage payment? Even if your child is not healed? Even if the college of your dreams turns down your scholarship application?

Knowing God is able to save and knowing He may choose a different plan is a difficult acknowledgement for the Christian striving to be obedient. Shadrach, Meshach, and Abednego's commitment to remain faithful, no matter the outcome, demonstrated their unconditional love for God and their total surrender to His plan.

And then we have Mary—unmarried and pregnant without "plausible" explanation—yet faithful to everything God asked her to do. Even if people gossiped behind her back, even if Joseph sometimes looked at her with a puzzled expression.

What difficulties are you facing today? What are you hoping God will save you from? I urge you to stand strong in your faith, knowing that the God who sent you a Savior on the first Christmas is still saving His people, day by day, in ways we can only imagine.

Tattered but Treasured

"Watch for this: A girl who is presently a virgin
will get pregnant. She'll bear a son and name him
Immanuel (God-With-Us)."

—ISAIAH 7:14 MSG

On Christmas Eve day in 1992, doctors gave little hope for
my grandfather's recovery. Mom called me, frantic. This
could be his last Christmas; we had to get a tree for his room!
The store shelves were nearly bare except for one small tree.

Just an old, tattered Christmas tree. If you saw it, you
would wonder why I've displayed it in a place of honor, close
to the dining room table where we all gather on Christmas
Day. Why is this the one tree I wouldn't trade for a million
dollars?

Because of the rest of the story. We smuggled our treasure
into Granddad's room. While Mother and I decorated the tree,
we played music, reminisced, laughed—and even shed a few
tears for all the great memories. I will never forget that day.

As it turned out, this wasn't Granddad's last Christmas
tree. He recovered. But my mother was diagnosed with cancer
the following February and was gone by April. My granddad's
tree turned out to be Mother's last tree.

*If your life took an unexpected turn—as it did for my mother
and grandfather and a Jewish girl named Mary—where would
you turn to find meaning? I hope your answer is, "Jesus."*

You're an Original

I praise you because I am fearfully
and wonderfully made.

—PSALM 139:14

received the best sweater for Christmas last year. Even the tag was cool. It said, "I am an original. I vary in color. I fade. I have pulls on me. I'm wrinkled in places I shouldn't be. But I am perfectly imperfect, intended to achieve this one-of-a-kind look."

Don't you love that! There's something special about owning a one-of-a-kind item. An original.

I was having a little sweater celebration when God interrupted. He said something like this: "Really! You're all excited because this sweater is an original? You sure don't get that excited about being an original yourself. You don't get so excited about *your* unique imperfections. You're faded in places. You've got a wrinkle here and there. You're perfectly imperfect. But I don't hear you celebrating *that*!"

God was right (He always is). Few of us ever celebrate the way we are. We all want to be better somehow. Being an original is good, but we'd prefer that our originality didn't include gray hair, wrinkles, that nervous giggle, or that short temper.

What would happen if you quit despising your flaws and uniqueness and started celebrating them? How would life be different if you looked in the mirror each morning and said, "I'm an original" and were glad about it.

Do You See the Light?

We know that in all things God works
for the good of those who love him, who have
been called according to his purpose.

—ROMANS 8:28

Does it sometimes feel as if no amount of Christmas lights can overcome the world's darkness? Maybe people felt the same way that first Christmas.

But Jesus entered that darkness—in person, as a baby. And that tells us there is hope.

God is present. He's Emmanuel: God is with us. Darkness cannot prevail against His light. Evil cannot triumph against His goodness. That's the promise of Christmas.

Do you love God? Have you surrendered control of your life to Him and asked Him to be your Savior? If so, everything going on in your life today—not some things, but everything; not just the good, but the difficult; not just the understand-able, but the things that make no sense—everything is going to work out for your good and God's glory.

Remember Rest?

"Oh, that I had the wings of a dove!
I would fly away and be at rest."

—PSALM 55:6

December is on its way out. You have survived the gift buying and the gift wrapping, the baking and the indulging, the school plays and the office parties, the tricky relatives and the … well, you probably don't want any more reminders!

Then you crawled out of bed this morning and saw all the post-season chores to be done. Don't do them! They will wait! Surprise yourself and your family with a lazy, do-nothing day.

Rest is one of the gifts God offers you today. Will you slow down enough to accept it? If you forget how to slow down, ask your Father to show you.

Look up "Boxing Day" using your favorite search engine or ask Siri for help. See what I mean? Today really is a holiday in many countries across the globe.

DECEMBER 27

A Time to Rebuild

"You see the trouble we are in. …
Come, let us rebuild."

—NEHEMIAH 2:17

Look around you.

What has been neglected? What needs repairing?

Where have troubles crept in and caused damage?

Has boredom invaded your marriage?

Has your office staff grown weary?

Have your neighbors become disconnected from one another?

Has your conversation with your teenager lost its way?

Now, imagine how things could be. Remember, a Savior has entered the world. He makes all things new. He brings healing and hope. With Him, nothing is impossible.

OK, now I'll ask you again. Imagine how things could be. Then, imagine one small step you can take today to inspire change.

What have you been putting off? I know what it's like to keep saying, "One day, God, one day." But ask yourself, Could one day be this day?

Gratitude Noted

I thank my God upon every remembrance of you.
—PHILIPPIANS 1:3 KJV

Looking back on the year, who are you thankful for? Who left an impact on you? Who inspired you with a fresh perspective when you needed it most? Who simply brightened your life with a smile?

Maybe you're thankful for those who taught your children. Or your pastor. A friendly neighbor. A coworker. Perhaps you'd like to give thanks for the people who serve you in small ways, like that diligent young man who changes the oil in your car.

Today, after you thank God for these people, why not write a short note of gratitude to a few of them? For all you know, they could be wondering if anything they did made a difference this past year. Your expression of thanks will assure them that they matter and will give a great jumpstart to their new year.

A Year of No Regrets

"If you knew the gift of God and who it is that
asks you for a drink, you would have asked him
and he would have given you living water."

—JOHN 4:10

When Jesus offered the Samaritan woman "living water,"
I wonder what she imagined that to be. Perhaps her
first hope was for an easier life. Home delivery of living water! No more daily treks to the well to face vulgar comments
and accusatory looks. Good thought, but no. Jesus had come
to offer so much more! He wanted to take the only "water"
she had—all that she considered vile, regretful, abusive, and
wasteful—and gift it with meaning and a purpose, if she
would allow Him. He had come—at the perfect time—not
to take away the life she had already endured, but to bring
significance to it.

What are you ashamed of in your life? What fills you with
regret about the year almost past? Today, ask Jesus to free you
from your regrets by pouring His living water into those areas
and showing you how they can be transformed. Thank Him
for the hope He offers you because of His transforming power.

Growing Wings

After you have suffered a little while,
[God] will himself restore you and make you strong.

—1 PETER 5:10

Earlier in the year, I wrote about how a butterfly begins as an ugly caterpillar, which, over time is transformed into a majestic butterfly—something completely new—because of what goes on *inside* the cocoon.* Perhaps you know that a butterfly that is released too soon from its cocoon cannot fly because its wings are underdeveloped.

We are like that butterfly. Sometimes struggles are exactly what we need in our lives. If God allowed us to go through our lives without any obstacles, it would cripple us. We would not be as strong as what we could have been. We could never fly.

Thank God today for something He has used in your life this past year to restore you, strengthen you, or prepare you for flight.

---

* See the July 9 devotional.

Memory Keeping

"Tell them to take up twelve stones …
to be a memorial."

—JOSHUA 4:3, 7

After safely crossing the Jordan, Joshua instructed twelve men to go back into the river and secure twelve stones. The urge to keep going into this new land must have been strong, but Joshua refused to push forward just yet. He insisted that everyone stop and remember and create a memorial to what God had done for them.

I hope you are anticipating a new year with hope and excitement. But before you forge ahead, why not stop and remember and create a memorial? Turn this into a family tradition as you pause together and recall blessings from each month of the year that's about to end. Then give thanks to God: It may not have always been an easy year, but it was a year in which He was always with you.

After talking about the ways God has blessed you this year, create a scrapbook or take some photos to document your family memorial.

About the Author

Kim Crabill is founder and president of Roses and Rainbows Ministries, Inc. and Community COFFEEs (Conversations of Friends of Faith to Encourage and Equip). She has traveled nationally for more than twenty years, speaking at retreats and conferences as well as to Bible study groups, and has been interviewed on national TV and radio.

Kim's message and passion come from her personal experience of longing to be used by God yet feeling unusable because of past abuse, anorexia, diet pill addiction, and depression. Her mother's deathbed challenge set Kim on the path of daring to be and do what God had purposed for her, a journey she wrote about in her book *Burdens to Blessings*. She is also author of *Burdens to Blessings: Young Adult Edition*, *Infinitely More: Your 40-Day Ephesians 3:20 Adventure*, *A Cup of Hope*, *A Cup of Freedom*, and *A Cup of Christmas*.

Kim is married to Lee Crabill and together they have two adult sons.

For more information about Kim Crabill and her ministries, visit rosesandrainbows.org.